AF478467

Humanism and Ideology

Humanism
and Ideology
An Aristotelian View

by

JAMES R. FLYNN

London and Boston
ROUTLEDGE & KEGAN PAUL

*First published 1973
by Routledge & Kegan Paul Ltd
Broadway House, 68–74 Carter Lane
London EC4V 5EL and
9 Park Street, Boston, Mass. 02108, U.S.A.
Printed in Great Britain by
Ebenezer Baylis & Son Ltd
The Trinity Press, Worcester, and London*

ISBN 0 7100 7442 5

TO VICTOR

*There is no country on earth which has more of a common, explicit
ideology—more of a common, explicit morality, I might say.
This is the old Enlightenment ideal: dignity of the human individual,
justice between people, liberty, equality of opportunity, and
brotherhood.*

Gunnar Myrdal, speaking of America

Contents

Acknowledgments

My debt to those whom I know only through their published works will emerge in the text. Among my lecturers, certain men did much to encourage my interest in political ethics, namely, Professors Leo Strauss, Martin Diamond, and most of all, Jerome Kerwin. Colleagues and scholarly correspondents who helped to develop my thinking include Professor J. G. A. Pocock, Father Benedict Ashley, James Thornton (in particular), and the late Professor E. A. Olssen. My thanks are due to Stanley I. Benn and Professor R. G. Durrant for a careful reading of various drafts of the manuscript. I owe much to the editor of this series, Professor D. Z. Phillips, whose criticism forced me to do the best work my talents and the present state of my knowledge permit.

An early version of Chapter 3 appeared in the *Australian Journal of Politics and History*; the author would like to thank the Editor for permission to reprint material taken from it.

1

The Problem of Ethical Scepticism

To deal with the problem of ethical scepticism, to show why it is of particular interest to political activists and students of politics, these are the principal aims of this book. This problem is variously called that of ethical truth versus ethical scepticism, value absolutism versus relativism, value objectivism versus subjectivism, etc., although, as we shall see, all of these terms will eventually be found wanting. However, to make a beginning, the problem might be described as this : Imagine that we are locked in debate with an opponent whose basic values differ from our own, let us say a Nietzschean, about whose way of life is best ; and assume that we want not only to defend our ideals but also to persuade uncommitted men, men who are genuinely torn between our ideals and his. Can we make a claim on behalf of our way of life fundamentally different from any claim he could advance, for example, a claim that our way of life was somehow valid even for those who did not champion it? In other words, how can we justify our basic ethical and political ideals against such an opponent, justify them perhaps not so much to him as to those who are as yet uncommitted. I will attempt to deal with this problem, but the reader should mark this : I promise no sure solution. What I will try to provide is a *hope* (albeit a hope that empirical evidence may prove to be in vain) of a semi-solution, words that will become clearer by the close of this work.

A word about the title, *Humanism and Ideology*. First, as a political philosopher, I am primarily interested in the clash of *ideologies* rather than the choices that confront individuals in everyday life. Therefore, my attempt to provide a solution to the problem of ethical scepticism will take place in the setting of ideological competition and will be heavily coloured by that context. Second, the way of life that I wish to justify against its ideological opponents is often called the *humanist* ideal. The content of the humanist ideal will be elaborated later on, but for now I will refer to it as a life of humane love and creative work. There are variations on the humanist ideal, of course, and I have selected out the Jeffersonian ideal, one that sets a high value on political freedom, as perhaps its highest expression. But I want to emphasize that I have selected Jeffersonianism primarily to add some specificity to the humanist ideal, primarily as a concrete example of what humanism ought to mean in a certain social setting, namely, that of America. I am well aware that political freedom has certain social prerequisites which to date are rarely present and that significant humanist experiments have taken place that give it a far less prominent role than Jeffersonianism does. To justify the humanist ideal is my major concern and I hope that no one will be distracted by the peculiar features of what is used mainly as an illustration of it.

As for the subtitle, 'an Aristotelian view', it reflects the fact that this work has a secondary purpose, a polemical, or to use a more respectable word, a pedagogical one. Perhaps the most exciting development in political ethics in recent years is the resurrection of schools. The traditional division of political thinkers into schools resulted from differing approaches to the problem of justifying their ideals (plus related differences over just whose ideals were capable of being justified), a problem that is essentially an epistemological one. But when intuitionism and emotivism came to dominate ethics (particularly in England) during the inter-war period, the schools went into decline, for now justifications of the traditional kind were thought to be either unnecessary or impossible or both. In this atmosphere, the rise of linguistic analysis bolstered the view that the traditional schools were passé: it was believed that as thinkers came to agree on the meaning of ethical propositions, they would also agree on the extent to which such propositions could be verified; which meant that thinkers would share a common position on the epistemology of ethics, on the problem of justification, thus leaving no reason to divide into schools. In fact, however, linguistic analysis has not brought unity on the epistemology of ethics. Beginning in the fifties, and particularly since 1960, thinkers have begun to divide in terms of their approaches to the problem of justification, a trend which has promoted discussion of substantive issues such as just what sort of life men ought to live. Schools that were bullied into a subterranean existence are beginning to re-emerge, to punch their way through linguistic analysis and come out on the other side, albeit altered because of the experience. I refer to the rise of Hare's neo-Kantianism, Mary Warnock's neo-utilitarianism and von Wright's neo-Hobbesian approach, the latter being combined with a strong humane commitment and a considerable debt to the ancients. I want to add neo-Aristotelianism to the lists, to show that a natural law approach is a viable contender in the post-analysis competition between the schools.

This polemical purpose helps to explain why I have chosen to deal with ethical scepticism, something that poses the problem of justifying one's ideals in its most acute form. For it is my view that neo-Aristotelianism can do more to clarify this problem than any of the other new schools and also, that no problem is of greater potential interest to students of politics, what with their often passionate commitment to certain ethical and political ideals. Indeed, it is hard to think of a problem better suited to convince students that ethical and political philosophy is relevant to the great issues of the day. To drive this point home, I have tried to dramatize the debate of ethical truth versus scepticism by putting it in an actual social setting, an American one, to demonstrate that flesh and blood men, struggling to effect actual social reforms, have found it of great importance. I have also tried to keep my style as non-technical as possible with the hope of being comprehensible to students nearing the end of an introductory course and the general educated public. Hopefully, however, the analysis has not emerged so simplified as to fail to interest my academic colleagues.

It was remarked above that all the new schools have been altered by the experience of absorbing the findings of linguistic analysis. The major adjustment I have found necessary in my brand of Aristotelianism is to purge it of its metaphysics, while salvaging the core of its conceptual approach to ethical and political problems. Thus, my analysis will involve no references to a transcendental realm, nor the positing of any entities beyond human experience, nor the making of any assertions of fact that cannot be tested empirically. It may be asked if, in view of this, I have the right to call myself a neo-Aristotelian or my approach that of natural law. In reply, I only know that the works of Plato and Aristotle, their concepts and vocabulary, took me into a world of distinctions far more helpful than anything I have encountered before or since, particularly when dealing with the agonizing problem of ethical scepticism.

The above purposes, particularly the pedagogical one, can be achieved only if certain common opinions, prejudicial both to my problem and my school, are overcome. It is often contended that the problem of ethical scepticism is not significant—or that if it is significant, it is best left unsolved in that a solution would promote intolerance—or that if it is to be solved, this will not be done by any variant of natural law. This last reflects the widely-held view that all naturalistic schools have been discredited, the view that both classical natural law (stemming from Plato and Aristotle) and modern natural right (stemming from Locke and Rousseau) can be lumped together for purposes of critique and shown to be guilty of muddled thinking at best and the naturalistic fallacy at worst. In view of all of this, I would like to postpone my actual attempt to use an Aristotelian approach to deal with the problem of ethical scepticism and spend the first four chapters of this work on the following tasks: (1) Clarifying the problem of ethical scepticism and showing why it *ought* to make a difference to politically committed men, particularly humane men—which will be attempted in this chapter plus the next; (2) showing that this problem *has* made a difference to politically committed men, namely, certain prominent Americans—Chapter 3; (3) refuting the contention that a solution to this problem ought to be feared by humane men as destructive of their ideals, a fear common in America—also in Chapter 3; (4) showing that the approach of natural law does *not* stand or fall with the doctrine of modern natural right, a doctrine open to devastating critique—Chapter 4.

*   *   *

Thus far, we have tried to clarify the problem of ethical truth versus scepticism by referring to a hypothetical dispute, a dispute between two men engendered by conflicting basic values. Here it is necessary to elucidate, the word 'basic', for men can fall into dispute about a *subordinate* question of value even though they share the same *basic* values. For example, two men may hotly dispute the rightness of capital punishment and then discover that what they really disagree about is whether or not it deters potential murderers. That is, one may think that it does and that the lives saved thereby outnumber those lost on the scaffold, while the other may think that it rarely deters anyone; but they may agree on the basic question of value that the prime objective should be to preserve human life as much as possible. In that case, their dispute can be resolved by settling a question of *fact*, by *evidence* as to whether capital punishment actually reduces the murder rate. Or another example, there may be a dispute about the desirability of socialized medicine. During the debate, it may become obvious that both disputants are humane, that both want their fellow men to live as felicitously as possible, but that one of them believes that whatever may be gained by more comprehensive medical care will be cancelled out by a loss of initiative, a loss that will encourage men to lapse into a languor which will rob them of happiness. Such a debate might then be resolved by settling questions of fact, such as whether or not the Swedes (who have socialized medicine) really show less initiative than Americans.

In these two examples then, the disputes were not really rooted in conflicting values; rather they were engendered by differing assumptions about facts or causes and effects. Thus, they were disputes about subordinate questions of value rather than basic ones, for the difference between these two is precisely that the former hinge on questions of fact while the latter do not (at least in any simple way). But what if our opponent in a dispute about capital punishment or socialized medicine *grants* all our factual evidence and still disagrees? What if he says, 'prevention of murder and preserving human life are all very well, but the relatives of the murdered man have a right to revenge', or if he says, 'most men can be as sick and miserable as misfortune allows for all I care, just so long as superior men are free to live as they please'? Then we would know that we were dealing with a man who could agree with us on all questions of fact, or at least on all ordinary facts (later on we will try to confront him with certain facts about human nature), and yet oppose us. For he has fundamentally non-humane values and therefore, the *very facts* that settle questions one way for us because of our humane values affect him in precisely the opposite way! On the level of ideological disputes, we often run into something similar, that is, an opponent who recommends to mankind a way of life we find abhorrent essentially because his basic values are opposed to our own, e.g. a Nazi. Or we can envisage ourselves in ideological debate with a Nietzschean, who would recommend a slavish life for the mass of men and the life of the superman for an élite.

This technique of clarifying the problem of ethical

scepticism by way of envisaging disputes engendered by conflicting basic values has recently come under attack as too artificial. The claim is that no actual dispute ever comes down merely to a conflict of values, that all actual disputes involve disagreement about facts as well and that the two sources of the dispute cannot be neatly disentangled. This objection seems to me quite to miss the point. Philosophers utilize hypothetical disputes, like those described above, neither because such disputes actually occur in pure form nor because they hope thereby to discover ways of actually resolving disputes (that is a job for educators, politicians, diplomats, and sometimes, sadly, armies). Rather, philosophers utilize them for two purposes: first, to illustrate what they mean when they say that we sometimes encounter men whose *basic* values differ from our own—and this, as we have seen, requires that all extraneous disagreements about facts be stripped away; and second, to show how hard it is to *justify* our basic ideals when faced with such persons, to focus on the peculiar problem of justification that a conflict of values, as distinct from a disagreement over facts, poses. Now certainly no one will deny that different men actually do have differing values; this comes out in all sorts of ways, both in disputes and other situations. And certainly no one will deny that the basic values of men are important both personally and politically, that men with opposing values will live differently and preach different ideologies. And finally, if our basic values are so significant, then the problem of justifying them may also be significant, as I hope to show.

While on the subject of the sort of disputes that pose the problem of justifying our fundamental ideals, recall that we are primarily interested in *ideological* disputes rather than those about *personal* ethics. Ideologies are complex things often involving a metaphysics, an epistemology, a theory of history, a theory about the roots of political authority, etc. But most ideologies also involve what I call ideological appeals, statements which claim that a certain way of life is better for mankind than other ways of life, statements that generate counter-claims and thus ideological disputes. Indeed, those of us who have lived through the cold war and suffered through the speeches of its statesmen have heard such claims almost daily on the international scene ; further, they are hardly absent from domestic politics, as we shall see when we take a look at the clash between Jeffersonians and conservative Social Darwinists in America. No doubt, when discussing the validity of these claims, we will incidentally shed some light (or dark) on the personal ethical problems of the disputants, such as how they should live. But again, our principal preoccupation will be with the validity of a disputant's ideological appeals, with whether or not it is *legitimate* for him to claim that his way of life is somehow best for mankind, perhaps even best for his opponent.

There is a complication here in that not all ideologues hold up their way of life as an ideal for *all* mankind. For example, racist ideologues (like the Nazis) and élitist ideologues (like Nietzsche) divide mankind into two ethical species, a fully human species and a sub-human one, and urge only the former to espouse their ideal way of life. It might be better to say that ideologues tend to claim that their way of life is best for either mankind or an élite sub-species of mankind. But this would be cumbersome, so I will stick to the simpler phrase and let the reader read in the qualification whenever appropriate.

* * *

Having clarified the nature of a dispute involving conflicting basic values, we can now analyse the difference between ethical truth and ethical scepticism. The believer in ethical truth, when faced with such a dispute, feels that he can fall back upon some method of gaining ethical knowledge, of establishing whose values are nearer the truth about good and evil, or at least, some method of determining whose values have objective or non-partisan status. Some believers in ethical truth turn to non-empirical methods, or better, methods distinct from those normally utilized by the natural or social sciences. On a simple level, a religious man may feel that an omniscient and benevolent God tells men, either through scripture or direct inspiration, what is truly good and evil; a Platonist may believe that dialectic allows one to plumb the contents of the Platonic Ideas and thus discover the perfect state of man and the nature of justice. Others turn to empirical tests, for example, an Aristotelian might feel that one could study mankind's experience with different ways of life over thousands of years and determine which of them perfected man's nature. However, what unites all believers in ethical truth is belief in their ability to make a case to this effect: that certain values or ideals are worthy of respect even from those who do *not* value them— that a certain way of life has objective or non-partisan status, *which is to say* that it has validity not only for its partisans (those who appreciate and champion it) but also for men who do *not* appreciate it and espouse some other way of life. Thus, they believe that their opponent, even though his basic values diverge from theirs, should concede that their values or way of life have a validity superior to his own.

In effect, believers in ethical truth hold that basic value disputes can be resolved, at least *in theory*. Whether they can be resolved in practice is another matter; one's opponent may be unable to understand the proper method, or be unable to gain access to the decisive evidence, or be too biased to assess the evidence properly, or just be too stubborn to give in when he knows he is wrong. Indeed, as far as practice goes, most believers in ethical truth would hold that ethical disputes are far more difficult to resolve than those about facts. What separates the believer from the sceptic is the question of resolvability in theory, for the ethical sceptic holds that basic value disputes are *inherently* unresolvable. The sceptic thinks that he can refute whatever arguments are presented in favour of revelation, or deductive demonstrations, or dialectic, or human experience, as a method of determining what values have objective status.

He concludes that when one is caught in a basic value dispute with an opponent, one can claim *no advantage* in terms of justification. If you claim that your values are self-justifying, he can claim the same. If you tell your opponent, let us say a realistic Social Darwinist, a man with a savagely competitive ideal and no factual illusions, that you abhor his values, he can say the same to you—and *that is that*! It is *this* about ethical scepticism, that it leaves your most cherished ideals on a par in terms of justification with an opponent's loathed ideals, which demoralizes so many men who are deeply committed to humane values.

I hope that it is now clear why deeply committed men are likely to react strongly to the sceptic's contention that basic value disputes cannot be resolved even in theory. For, as long as one believes in ethical truth, lack of resolvability in practice may prove frustrating but it poses no direct threat to one's *esprit de corps*. It merely means (as above) that your opponent suffers from some obvious defect which prevents him from seeing that you are right about whose way of life possesses objective validity ; indeed, his blindness may merely mean that *he* knows less about the value of his way of life, *vis-à-vis* yours, than *you* do. But none of this alters the fact that you can know that you are right in such a dispute. While, if the sceptic is correct, *no one* in such a dispute can claim superior status for his values ; it is this that disturbs deeply committed men so. Unless you are naïve, you do not hope to come out of a dispute with a Nazi, or a Nietzschean, or a Social Darwinist having actually convinced him that your values are worthy of his regard. But what if you must grant that you cannot make a case convincing *even to yourself* that your basic values possess a superior status, possess a status superior to the partisan validity that he can claim for his values?

I want to emphasize that the above analysis of the nature and significance of ethical scepticism is incomplete. It is intended to be provocative rather than definitive and presents primarily my conclusions rather than my reasons for those conclusions. The latter will be forthcoming, but the reader must wait until the end of the next chapter to see them fully spelled out. For now, I will merely attempt to avoid a few misconceptions and list some outstanding problems.

Concerning the psychological consequences of scepticism : nothing said thus far should be taken to deny that a dedicated man who becomes a sceptic can remain deeply committed to his ideals. If his upbringing and experience have inculcated in him a passionate concern for certain ideals, he is likely to remain a strong partisan on their behalf, whether he believes in ethical truth or not. I have been merely trying to explain why scepticism may affect his *esprit de corps* ; for certainly, it is often the most intense partisan of a certain way of life who most craves a non-partisan justification of it.

Concerning the logical consequences of scepticism, a major problem is to find an acceptable phrase for the value status it entails. William James, as we shall see, said that the sceptic must think of his ideals as being '*good* only for him' (and his fellow partisans). This wording is risky in that it is likely to suggest that he must use words like 'good' and 'evil' to praise or condemn *only* himself plus those who share his values and *not* his opponents. And such a suggestion is quite mistaken. If you become a sceptic, you can go right on condemning your opponent and he you ; you need merely concede that there is no reason why your opponent should *share* your condemnation of him or *give up* his condemnation of you. As the reader may have noticed, I have eschewed James's phrase for another, that is, I prefer to say that the sceptic must think of his ideals as '*valid* only for him' (and his fellow partisans). But this too has its drawbacks. We normally use the word 'valid' rather like the word 'true', i.e. to imply objective status ; for example, an argument which is valid is valid for everyone, not just some. Thus, to say 'valid for him' seems incoherent. However, I hope to convince my philosophical colleagues of two things : first, that using the word 'valid' has certain advantages, advantages which will become clear when we discuss whether scepticism entails nihilism ; and second, that if we are to use the word at all, we will be *compelled* to use phrases like 'valid for him' to describe what scepticism entails. After all, if I am correct, the sceptic must grant that his basic values lack objective status, that they are not worthy of regard from those who do not share them; which means that they are worthy of regard *only* from himself and his partisans.*

Although conceptually distinct, the logical and psychological consequences of ethical scepticism are causally interrelated and this engenders a further complication. I have just said that the phrase 'valid for him' makes sense *if* I am correct about what scepticism entails. Much the same is true of my thesis that loss of *esprit de corps* is a reasonable psychological reaction to scepticism. There are thinkers who embrace scepticism and yet, suffer no loss of *esprit de corps* despite what is obviously a deep commitment to their basic values. The explanation for this is what one would expect: they deny that the absence of a truth test of their basic values leaves them on a par in terms of justification with their opponents. To be specific, although they cannot prove that their ideals are worthy of regard from their opponents, they deny that this entails giving up claims to that effect. Clearly, we must eventually give these thinkers our full attention. And clearly, this will allow us to clarify certain terms used uncritically up to now, terms like 'objective status' and '*esprit de corps*'.

*   *   *

Let us begin our attempt to clarify the significance of ethical scepticism with a less demanding but necessary task. We must deal with certain misconceptions which are both mischievous and widespread, indeed, as far as students are concerned, these more than anything else tend to cloud the distinction between the believer in ethical truth and the sceptic.

* For those who find themselves unsatisfied even at the close of this work, I have added an appendix on the problem of 'valid for him'.

First, the believer in ethical truth does not have to hold that certain set patterns of behaviour should be followed no matter what the circumstances, that certain rules of conduct are *uniformly applicable* in all situations. There are many well-intentioned people who believe that one must never lie (as Kant did) or must always come to the aid of the distressed (as Don Quixote did). But most thinkers agree that the actor's situation should be taken into account, that is, they reject some rigid set of 'thou shalt nots' in favour of *flexibility*. For example, it is normally wrong to lie, but most humane men would have told a falsehood to save a Jew from the Nazis. On the domestic scene, where the U.S. government is overwhelmingly powerful measured against a few criminals, it is normally right to use force to rescue a kidnapped child. But on the international scene, those who suggested that America should use force to rescue 'captive nations', e.g. Hungary or Czechoslovakia, from Russia were ignoring the realities of the situation. America and Russia are approximately equal in nuclear power and any such step would have brought a nuclear war destructive of the U.S., the U.S.S.R., and the 'captive nation' as well, hardly a humane service to the latter. In sum, most humane men try to be realistic in pursuit of their ideals ; and certainly, they can exhibit a realistic flexibility whether they feel they can justify their basic values against ideological opponents or not. The description of ethical truth versus scepticism as a matter of ethical absolutism versus 'relativism' is deceptive here : the latter term gives the impression that the believer in ethical truth cannot vary his conduct *relative* to the situation.

These terms, abolutism versus relativism, also promote another misconception, namely, that the believer in ethical truth must hold that at least his basic ideals are *final* and *certain*, this time the word 'absolutism' (which calls up the notion of *absolute* truths) being the culprit. Certainly many thinkers who believed in ethical truth were absolutists ; the early Plato, Kant, and many theologians speak as if there are certain truths about good and evil which are both beyond doubt and constitute the last word. But note that these are thinkers who have espoused non-empirical roads to ethical truth. If a thinker utilizes an empirical method, he may assess the relevant evidence and come up with only a *probable* and *tentative* hypothesis. For example, an Aristotelian like myself looks upon all of history as a human experiment, as something which reveals the various ways of life possible for man and the extent to which these ways of life have perfected their practitioners. On the basis of this evidence, I would assert only that a certain way of life seems *most likely* to perfect man among those attempted *thus far*. I would leave open two possibilities : that evidence from the past which had escaped my attention might be cited in favour of one of the ways of life rejected as inferior ; and that men in the future might hit upon a way of life that brings human nature to an even greater degree of perfection. In other words, an empiricist's conception of ethical knowledge may well be like the usual conception of scientific knowledge of facts, that evidence can resolve basic disputes but only on a probable and tentative basis.*

A third misconception can be best avoided by keeping in mind the distinction between the content and status of our ethical and political ideals. An ethical sceptic *need not* be committed to non-humane or vicious values as far as the *content* of his ideals is concerned. He can be a humane man who is convinced that his values have only non-objective or partisan *status*, who is convinced that he can make no case that those who fail to share his humane ideals should grant them a validity superior to that possessed by their own (non-humane) ideals. Indeed, many ethical sceptics live humane, even heroic, lives. On the other hand,

* This paragraph is likely to put the reader off. The notion of viewing history as a 'human experiment', as a series of tests that reveal the potentialities of human nature and indicate which way of life is best for man, may seem both odd and barren. After all, will not each man assess history in terms of his own peculiar values? Does not my talk of 'perfecting man' imply that I hold some criterion of human perfection which is exempt from (or incapable of) empirical testing? The reader must be patient; Chapter 5 will clarify what I mean by the human experiment.

a believer in ethical truth can have vicious values. For example, Social Darwinists with quite inhumane values often believe that the way of life they espouse has objective status, that is, they believe it is worthy of regard by all mankind including those who loathe it.

A final point having to do with what is meant by ethical scepticism concerns mainly my own use of the words. It is possible for a thinker to hold that we can make a case that a certain way of life has objective validity in terms of one form of goodness but not in terms of other forms; indeed, this is my own view. The various forms of goodness will be carefully distinguished later on; for now, I will merely note that men use the word 'good' in a number of very different ways, that is, they may use it to mean pleasant (hedonic goodness), or felicitous (eudemonic goodness), or moral (moral goodness—what one ought to do). I intend to call a thinker a believer in ethical truth if he holds that a case can be made for objective validity in terms of *any one* of these forms of goodness, and to reserve 'ethical sceptic' for those who hold that *no* such case can be made. I feel that this usage is appropriate and not merely a matter of my own predilections: virtually every thinker who has ever tried to make a case for objectivity in ethics has relied primarily on one form of goodness, e.g. Kant relied on duty or moral goodness, Aristotle on happiness or eudemonic goodness, etc.; if we began to eliminate such thinkers from the ranks of those who are believers in ethical truth, it is hard to see who would be left!

On the other hand, merely that the great thinkers of the past were satisfied with a case in terms of one form of goodness does not mean that we can rest easy, for they often tended to overlook the limits on the significance of such a case. We must face up to these limits. In particular, as an Aristotelian, I must face up to the limits of a case made only in terms of happiness or eudemonic goodness. At first glance, these may seem to be so great as to be crippling. Are there not men who care little about happiness? Even if most men do care, what sort of person will be won over by a eudemonic appeal—will he not be among the worst of men, an unworthy convert willing to sell out his ideals in return for happiness? I will not evade such questions; much of the last chapter of this book is devoted to them. At that time, it will be conceded that a case for objective validity in terms of eudemonic goodness falls short of the full case for ethical truth a humane ideologue would like to have. But it will also be argued that such a case is not to be despised, that even a partial solution to an agonizing problem (the problem of ethical scepticism) may seem very precious.

In sum, note that virtually all of the traditional terms used to refer to our problem can get us into trouble. We have seen the dangers of speaking of 'absolutism versus relativism'. We can now see that even using 'ethical truth versus scepticism' could be deceptive, for it might give the impression that the sceptic can be refuted in terms of *all* of the forms of goodness. Soon we will find fault with 'objectivism versus subjectivism'. However, it might appear pedantic to drop the traditional terms for new ones; it is better to go on using them and guard against their dangers by way of a clear understanding of what our problem really entails.

*   *   *

While listing things which tend to obscure the significance of ethical scepticism, we cannot ignore the role of the 'matter of taste' analogy. This analogy asserts that the ethical sceptic must treat his value judgments as if they were mere whims or tastes. Its frequent use and abuse tended, until recently, to colour the whole debate about the significance of ethical scepticism: those who believed scepticism significant seemed to feel they had to show that it entailed treating *all* value judgments (however important) as if they were like tastes *in every way*; and those who thought scepticism not significant seemed to feel themselves vindicated if they could show that, sceptics or not, *some* of their assessments (however trivial) were unlike tastes *in any way*. An excellent example of the latter is T. D. Weldon whose book, *The Vocabulary of Politics*, retains something of the status of a text in many political science departments despite critical battering at the hands of philosophers. Weldon accuses the champions of objectivism in ethics of trying to frighten us by brandishing the taste analogy. He promises to show that we need not be afraid, that he for one can reject objectivism and not be reduced to discussing the goodness of slavery in the same way he would discuss the goodness of peppermint creams, namely, by saying that some enjoy them and some do not.[1] He makes much the same point about Hitler's concentration camps.[2]

The interesting thing in Weldon is how few of these promises are kept and how little space is devoted to those that are kept. There is no discussion of the goodness of slavery whatsoever and only a few scattered paragraphs on concentration camps.[3] But we get a very detailed discussion of why Weldon believes it absurd to say that all of his assessments are merely matters of taste. He tries to show that he has no difficulty in assessing secretaries (they must be hard-working and honest) or accountants (who must be able to add up figures correctly); he also indicates how we can assess statesmen, namely, a good statesman must deal effectively with the problems that affect his people, keep the confidence of his contemporaries, avoid revolution, and not blunder into a losing war.[4] None of this seems to me to have anything to do with the problem of justification which tends to disturb the humane sceptic. Of course, men can agree, whether they are humane or not, whether they are sceptics or not, on how to assess secretaries or even a statesman, if they limit themselves in the case of the latter to assessing his performance as a craftsman or technician. What pains the humane sceptic is his inability to resolve *certain disputes*, ideological disputes engendered by conflicting values. I refer to the sort of dispute we have with someone who agrees with us about assessing secretaries but wants a good secretary to engage more effectively in cut-throat economic competition. Or the sort of dispute we have with an opponent after we agree that Hitler was a competent diplomat (at least until he blundered into a losing war) and get down to arguing about whether someone ought to have served the German people as a good statesman given their tendencies in 1938. Faced with such disputes, the common ground we share with our opponents about assessing technical skills is not going to provide much solace.

This is not to say that I am criticizing Weldon for searching for common ground. I am criticizing him for emphasizing common ground of the most trivial kind; and I am suggesting that the reason he does this is because he is obsessed with discrediting the matter of taste analogy. As we have seen, it is always in order to determine whether or not we share certain values with our ideological opponents. If I were faced with opponents who endorsed slavery or concentration camps, I would attempt to divide them into two sorts. First, there are those whose basic values are not vicious but who believe in absurd racial theories. An opponent of this sort might say that Negroes are genetically inferior and are better off under a master whose mature reason and will can substitute for their immature faculties. Or he might believe that Jews are out to inflict some great evil on mankind and that they must be exterminated before they succeed. Clearly my disputes with these men are about subordinate questions of value and can be settled by factual evidence, although I might well suspect that their ready acceptance of such racial theories betokened some rather vicious values to which they were unwilling to admit. Second, my opponents might be of a sort who hold a savagely competitive ideal, for example, they might believe that success in war determines a people's merits and that the losers deserve whatever they get. In such a case, there is a basic clash of values and the problem of scepticism arises. Even then, a humane sceptic can test how seriously his opponents take their ideal by challenging them to be consistent about it, that is, he can ask them if they think it morally permissible for an enemy to exterminate them were they to lose a war. I will leave serious scrutiny of this kind of argument until we reach Hare, a thinker who makes use of it, rather than deal with it under Weldon, who does not. For now, I will merely say that if our opponents do not believe in racial myths, they are unlikely to feel at a loss.

Weldon's neglect of ideological disputes is too striking to be accidental; it is quite clear that he considers them peripheral to his main theme. There is only one to which he gives serious attention, that is, he devotes three pages to whether British democracy is superior to Russian Communism. His analysis runs essentially along these lines: (1) He outlines a humane-libertarian criterion which condemns censorship, intolerance of criticism, and travel restrictions; (2) he adds the supplementary criterion that the people living under the regime (particularly educated and sophisticated people who can assess it properly) must approve of it; and (3) he then grants that these criteria are only his personal ones and may be rejected by anyone who disagrees!—though he says his opponent's conflicting criteria must be 'equally usable' and quotes Mill for support, the famous passage that the only evidence we have that something is desirable is that people actually desire it.[5] These few pages stand as the exception which proves the rule. Even when Weldon does consider an ideological dispute, he misses just what the problem of ethical scepticism is all about. Note his casual admission that his criteria have only personal or partisan validity. Such a concession gives the whole game away, concedes precisely what so many of us find it so difficult to concede to the sceptic! In view of this, the reference to Mill is tantalizing, for Mill's argument is one that can be developed into an interesting (though in my opinion defective) attempt to escape the sceptic. However, Weldon makes no such attempt. Again, I believe that we see here the influence of the taste analogy. It lures Weldon into focusing on *its* validity, rather than the validity of his basic values; which means that it lures him into ignoring the real problem of justification which scepticism poses.

*   *   *

Leaving Weldon behind, what about the merits of the taste analogy? Does it clarify the significance of ethical scepticism to say that it entails treating our values (or at least our *basic* values) as if they were matters of taste? To anticipate: this analogy is deceptive and dangerous when used naïvely (as it most often is); but when used in a more sophisticated way, it is harmless and has a certain utility as a dramatic device.

The naïve users of the taste analogy use it to assert that someone who becomes an ethical sceptic should, if he is logically consistent, become a *nihilist*. They argue that the humane sceptic, for example, should *discount* his most cherished ideals and most passionate moral commitments; that he should look upon them as *illusory*, as things that have no real right to influence his conduct, as things no more significant to him than his most trivial whims or tastes. In this, they are simply mistaken; they have fallen into a fundamental confusion about what is at stake in the debate over ethical scepticism. For that debate is essentially about whether or not we can find a philosophically defensible test which will allow us to distinguish values with objective status from those with merely subjective status. Now if the sceptic is right, there is *no such test*; and therefore, no man's ideals need be discounted as subjective, as *not even worth the value he places upon them*. For that is really what the above users of the taste analogy are telling the sceptic he must do: that he must treat his values as illusory, treat them like *hallucinations*, like something that *has flunked* a test of objectivity and therefore must be discounted (just as hallucinations are discounted *vis-à-vis* veridical sense experience). But again, if the sceptic is right, the realm of value differs from that of fact precisely in the absence of such a test, so there is nothing in the realm of value analogous to either a veridical sense experience or a hallucination.

What ethical scepticism really means is this: we can neither say that our values have objective status, that they are worthy of regard from those who do not share them, *nor* say that they have subjective status, that they are *less* worthy of our regard than some other values we lack. Indeed, it means that our values are worth precisely *what they are worth to us*, and that may be a great deal, if we are passionately committed. If we become sceptics, we do have to grant that our basic values have only personal or partisan or non-objective validity—and, as we have seen, our inability to provide a supra-personal justification for them may be a blow to our *esprit de corps*. But we are not faced with nihilism, that is, we are not logically remiss for fighting on for our ideals as *fierce partisans*. We can now perceive the trap in describing ethical truth versus scepticism as objectivism versus 'subjectivism'. The latter term suggests that the sceptic must treat his values as *subjective*, as if they were somehow illusory.*

In order to avoid this trap, I will adopt the term 'non-objective' to describe the status which ethical scepticism entails for human values. And to drive the point home, to emphasize that the sceptic's ideals are still worth whatever they are worth to him, I will say that his values possess a certain sort of validity—that his values are 'worthy of regard by him' or 'valid for him', despite the eccentricity of this use of the word 'valid' (see p. 11). It will, of course, always be necessary to add that they are not objectively valid, that they are *not* worthy of regard by those who do not hold them.

In sum, the naïve users of the taste analogy are not so much following their analogy as deviating from it. For what characterizes trivial tastes is precisely that no test of objectivity or subjectivity is possible. And therefore, we do not discount our tastes in candy, etc., as worth less than they

---

* Some have argued that ethical scepticism is a loaded term in that 'scepticism' is often identified with nihilism. Therefore, they have suggested calling the philosophical debate 'ethical objectivism versus subjectivism' and discussing whether the latter entails 'scepticism', rather than (as I have done) calling it 'ethical truth versus scepticism' and discussing whether the latter entails 'nihilism'. As the reader can now see, I have not taken this suggestion because 'subjectivism' seems to me to be the loaded term, one that often deceives students into assuming that rejecting the possibility of a case for ethical truth entails nihilism. However, I certainly do not want to load the verbal dice and am happy to have the reader read 'subjectivist' and 'scepticism' for my 'sceptic' and 'nihilism' if he finds it helpful.

mean to us ; we treat them as worth *exactly that*. Similarly, the sceptic need not treat his ethical and political ideals as no more significant than his tastes unless that is how he actually feels about them.

We must not, however, conclude our indictment of those who abuse the taste analogy at this point. They are quite capable of leading us into a second confusion, almost as serious as the nihilist confusion, and again, the culprit is their claim that the sceptic must reduce all of his value judgments to the lowest common denominator (i.e. to the level of simple hedonic assessments). For if *all* value judgments is meant to include *moral* judgments (assessments about what we *ought* to do, our duties), such a claim tends to obscure something important about moral judgments— something which differentiates them from hedonic judgments (assessments about what we enjoy) whether we are sceptics or not. I refer to the fact that we must *give reasons* for our moral judgments, or better, that we must give reasons when we seem to be unwilling to *universalize* them. Hare calls this the rule of universalizability and suggests that the humanist can use it as a powerful weapon in ideological debate. I am less optimistic than he, but I do not deny that it is significant. Which elucidates why the above abuse of the taste analogy can be so serious : it can cause us to overlook something we can use in ideological debate *even if* we become sceptics.

Hare argues that universalizability is a defining characteristic of moral judgments ; I think that he is correct (although I do not think it is the sole defining characteristic). As for what it is all about, first and foremost, it is a principle of *logical consistency*. Assume that I did a certain act yesterday and then do that same act today. I must either give moral praise to both or condemn both—*if* I grant that the circumstances were the same in both cases, not exactly the same of course, but the same in terms of those circumstances deemed relevant to the morality of actions by my criteria. In other words, if I want to praise the first and condemn the second, I must give reasons and these reasons must focus on some difference in the circumstances (albeit those circumstances which I myself designate as relevant). However, the rule of universalizability consists of more than this (after all, we can be logically consistent about our likes and dislikes). It also includes being consistent when assessing *various actors*. That is, I must pass the same moral judgments on the actions of other persons that I pass on my own actions or give reasons, reasons of the sort described above. In other words, I cannot apply my moral criteria to only my own actions; I must be willing to apply them to the actions of others. And this last is not true of simple hedonic assessments. In that realm, the mere fact that an action is done by another is a good enough reason for not applying my taste criteria to it.

No doubt, this difference between moral judgments and hedonic judgments requires illustration. If a man approves of himself for doing a generous act under circumstances in which he has nothing to gain thereby and in which his motivation is love for another, he must also call such an act morally good when done by his worst enemy. Most of us are intuitively aware of this. Note that on those occasions when we are loath to grant an accolade, we tend to search for differences in the actor's circumstances which we deem morally relevant. For example, in the case of our worst enemy, we might claim that he knew the loan would be repaid with interest or that he was motivated by guilt. Also note that when we fail to do this, fail to explain away inconsistencies in the use of our criteria, we suffer a heavy penalty, namely, others can accuse us of not being serious about our ideals. Indeed, if we arbitrarily refuse to praise a man who is generous, others are likely to say: 'I thought you were *serious* about valuing generosity; but here is a generous man and yet, you refuse to praise him.' I wish to underline this last: Hare's opponents often emphasize that the rule of universalizability is merely a logical rule and not a moral principle; true, but what do we think of someone who is not even willing to be consistent about his moral principles?

Still in the moral realm, if someone says it is permissible for him to kill and eat his neighbour when that is the least expensive way to secure a dinner, he must also grant that it is morally permissible for his neighbour to devour him under the same circumstances (unless he can cite a criterion which discriminates between himself and his neighbour— as we shall see). However, when we move over to the realm of hedonic assessments things are different; we need *not* apply our own criteria to the actions of others. If a man says that he would *enjoy* eating his neighbour, it would make no sense to tell him that he must also assert that his neighbour would enjoy eating him. It would make sense to assert the latter only if his neighbour shares his taste for human flesh. But then, it is a case in which our man's criterion and his neighbour's criterion coincide; it is *not* a matter of our man universalizing his criterion so as to apply it to his neighbour's eating activities as well as his own.

Essentially, the rule of universalizability comes down to this: the logically consistent application of our moral criteria to the actions of others as well as our own. As for its utility in ideological debate, Hare tries to use it to force men with vicious ideals to contradict their moral principles, or reveal themselves as 'fanatics', or (besieged by contradictions) give up their moral vocabulary entirely.[6] He does not claim that he could do this in every case, but still he carries this use of the rule of universalizability much further than I can accept.[7] It is worth noting that even if Hare were successful, certain non-humane ideologues would not find his third alternative so unpalatable. For example, Nietzscheans voluntarily reject moral goodness and go to mankind with the message that their ideal way of life maximizes joy. They are only too happy to give up moral language and would look upon this as no penalty at all. However, let us put the best face possible upon the rule of universalizability as a weapon against non-humane ideologues by focusing on one who respects moral goodness, let us say a Social Darwinist who (like the Nietzschean) espouses a competitive ideal but who (unlike the Nietzschean) *wants* to tell mankind that it is at least morally permissible to live in accord with his ideal.

Our Social Darwinist will have two things in common with his fellows: first, he classifies men into at least two types, one of which deserves to triumph and the other of which deserves to lose, be exploited, die out, be exterminated, etc.; second, he endorses a competitive system designed to give victory to the former and defeat to the latter (which system may or may not be supposed to exist). When faced with the rule of universalizability, he will use his criterion of classification as a rebuttal. Imagine that we say to him: 'You assert that there is nothing immoral about a system in which you triumph and your neighbour goes under; would you say the same about a system in which your neighbour had the upper hand and you went under?' Our Social Darwinist will reply: 'I certainly would not. My neighbour deserves to go under because he is black, lazy, weak, philistine, materialistic, etc.; while I am white, hardworking, masterful, artistic, non-materialistic, etc.' In other words, he will answer us by citing a criterion of human merit in terms of which he and his sort *deserve* victory and others *deserve* defeat.

However, the debate need not end at this point. If our Social Darwinist is a *racist*, we can still use the rule of universalizability against him with great effect, as Hare convincingly shows.[8] For example, assuming he says *black* men should go under, we can ask him if he would say the same if we sneaked a pill in his food which turned his skin permanently black. Our opponent is now in a difficult position. The key to his difficulty is this: under these conditions, he can imagine himself turning black without any change in the *sort of man* he is, without any change in his character, values, record of achievement, etc. Despite this, he can still give an affirmative answer to our question, of course; but only at the price of holding that everything save colour is irrelevant, that all he has done and all he has become are irrelevant to his merits. He is unlikely really to believe this or convince others, particularly those who admire him for his *personal qualities*, the very qualities he now calls irrelevant. Hare labels a man who gives an affirmative answer a 'fanatic'. I object to this term, but I am quite willing to grant that such a man has been effectively emasculated as an ideologue. And that is why virtually all racists are unwilling to make colour their criterion of human merit; instead they assert a *correlation* between colour and certain personal traits which do count as criteria, that is, they assert that black men are by nature lazy, vicious, stupid, slavish, etc. But then, we can refute them by presenting factual evidence to the contrary.

We can now appreciate the principal utility of the rule of universalizability: it can force racists to bring their absurd factual hypotheses into the open where they can be refuted. However, before we rejoice too much at routing our opponent, we must note two things. First, keep in mind *iust why* he was so vulnerable, namely, because he cited *colour* as a criterion of human merit or at least, assumed a correlation between colour and certain personal traits. The situation may be very different when we run into an opponent who cites *personal traits* as his criterion and does not assume a correlation between those traits and skin-colour. Second, the fact that our opponent must give up racial myths does not mean he has any reason to respect humane ideals. If he really holds a savagely competitive ideal, he will merely be willing to admit black men as competitors on an equal footing. I fear that we will still find much to condemn in a Social Darwinist who has given up his racism.

Let us go on to take a look at a second opponent. After all, there are legions of Social Darwinists who do not espouse a racist criterion of human merit. Rather, they cite certain personal qualities, that is, they believe that tough, predatory, hard-working types should triumph and that weak, soft-hearted, 'lazy' types should go under. We can, of course, try the same tactic we did with the racist: just as we asked him to imagine himself as black, we can ask our new opponent to imagine himself with the values and traits of those he condemns and to tell us whether he, under those circumstances, should go under. But now the argument just will not work: the racist could imagine himself turning black *without* any real alteration in the sort of man he was; while the non-racist can imagine himself like those he condemns *only by* imagining himself changed into the sort of man he loathes (only by thinking of himself as weak, soft-hearted, etc.). Thus, the non-racist will not hesitate to give us an affirmative answer. He will say: 'Certainly, I believe that I ought to go under when I imagine myself like that lot; though I do wish to remind you that I am not *in fact* like that at all.' Indeed, he will be consistency itself in regard to various actors, that is, he will willingly say: 'I do not merely praise *myself* when I act to exploit the weak and soft-hearted; I am more than happy to praise *them* when they do something which helps send themselves under.'

We do not need to draw upon hypothetical opponents in order to find examples of non-humane ideologues willing to universalize their ideals. A recent event provides an excellent (and rather chilling) example, namely, the killing of a Japanese-American surgeon by a hippie ideologue. The hippie did not do it because the surgeon was yellow-skinned (and thus avoids our pill); he did not do it because he believed yellow skin to be correlated with certain personal traits (and thus avoids evidence to the contrary). According to his manifesto, he did it because the surgeon was a materialist; and this is a fact which, given the victim's life-style, seems difficult to challenge. As for asking him to imagine himself a materialist, here again our opponent can do this only by imagining himself very much changed, changed into the sort of man he loathes. Certainly, he would answer: 'Me, a hippie, turned into a materialist; I would deserve death and nothing less.' Precisely because he is in fact so much a non-materialist, he is happy to universalize the principle that all materialists should be exterminated—for that principle does not *really* require that *his* sort of man should go under.

*   *   *

Our indictment of the naïve users of the matter of taste analogy is now complete: they tempt us to think that an ethical sceptic cannot take his ideals seriously; and they encourage us to overlook something important about our moral ideals, namely, that if we *do* take them seriously, we must universalize them.

However, despite the importance of the rule of universalizability, we must not forget that it is no substitute for a case for objective status: it just *does not solve* the problem of justification which ethical scepticism poses. The amoral Nietzschean is exempt from it. As for Social Darwinists, it is primarily effective only against racists and even they need merely give up their racial myths, that is, they need not grant that our humane ideals are worthy of their regard. Our ideological opponents can be as non-humane as they please and still universalize their ideals, witness our 'anti-materialist'. No one moral code is uniquely universalizable. And once our opponent has universalized his basic ideals, we can claim *no advantage* over him in terms of justification— as long as we remain sceptics.

This last makes one sympathetic to at least some of the users of the taste analogy. The more sophisticated among them did not really mean that the sceptic must treat all of his ideals as analogous to simple hedonic assessments. They used the taste analogy as a dramatic device, as a way of bringing home why being on a par (in terms of justification) with a non-humane opponent causes them so much pain. They used it to say, 'how can you bear to be at as much of a loss in a dispute about your basic values as you are in a dispute about tastes?' And this, it seems to me, is something well worth dramatizing.

NOTES

[1] T. D. Weldon, *The Vocabulary of Politics* (London: Penguin Books, 1953), pp. 13–14.

[2] *Ibid.*, pp. 147–8.

[3] *Ibid.*, pp. 16, 99.

[4] *Ibid.*, pp. 151–4, 165–70.

[5] *Ibid.*, pp. 175–7.

[6] R. M. Hare, *Freedom and Reason* (London: Oxford University Press, 1963), pp. 90–111, 157–73.

[7] *Ibid.*, pp. 173–85.

[8] *Ibid.*, pp. 203–24.

2

The Significance of Ethical Scepticism

We cannot yet abandon the problem of the significance of ethical scepticism, if only because so many thinkers disagree so strongly with my views. Like a good Aristotelian, I try to chart a middle course and just as there are those who attack me for attaching too little importance to scepticism (namely, those who believe it entails nihilism), there are others who criticize me for attaching too much. These latter challenge my assertion that scepticism means our basic values possess only non-objective or partisan status, that it means our ideals are valid for or worthy of regard from only ourselves and our partisans. They grant they are sceptics in a certain sense, that is, they feel unable to go beyond their basic values and offer a case or proof that those values are worthy of regard from their opponents (they call such a case one external to their values). However, they refuse to grant that their inability to offer *a proof* of this sort entails giving up *the claim* that their values are worthy of regard from all mankind—entails giving up claims to what I call objective status. Many of them, though not all, cite Wittgenstein as the source of their views on this question.

While Wittgenstein's writings on ethics are fragmentary and scattered, it is easy to see why his name is cited particularly if we focus on his 'Lecture on Ethics'. Here he identifies the *ethical* use of good, right, etc., with using them in an *absolute* sense.[1] Translated into my language,

30

this becomes identifying the *moral* use of value terms with using them in an *objective* sense. Unlike myself, Wittgenstein uses 'ethical' as a synonym for 'moral', rather than as a broader term inclusive of non-moral forms of goodness. As for using value terms in an 'absolute sense', he makes it clear this means claiming that others should respect your basic values whether they actually do so or not, that your ideals are worthy of regard by everyone in a way 'independent of his tastes and inclinations'[2]—the resemblance to what I call 'objective status' is obvious enough. Wittgenstein makes it equally clear that he holds no hope of making a case that certain ideals possess objective status, indeed, he calls such a notion a chimera.[3] This, of course, immediately raises the question of whether he thought we have the right to go on claiming our ideals possess objectivity in the absence of such a case. Rush Rhees, on the basis of conversations with him and an analysis of his writings, is convinced that he did.[4] This conviction seems plausible in the light of Wittgenstein's remarks, both in his 'Lecture' and in conversation with Friedrich Waismann, that he has the highest regard for those who use value terms in an absolute sense.[5]

The question of what views Wittgenstein held is secondary. What is of interest is that so many of those influenced by him are convinced that ethical scepticism poses no threat to their *esprit de corps*. They reason as follows: 'First, moral assessments by their very nature involve a claim that our basic values are worthy of regard from all mankind, as a look at the form and usage of moral propositions will show. Such propositions are often stated in the form "*Men should* do such and such", a phrasing which implies that the behaviour recommended is worthy of regard from all men. Concerning usage, consider what we do when confronted with an opponent who refuses to accept a recommendation on the grounds that his basic values differ from our own. If the recommendation is non-moral in character, e.g. that he should learn to play tennis really well, we are inclined to let the matter drop and merely tell him he is missing something. But if the recommendation is a moral one, e.g. that he should behave more humanely towards his friends, we do not let the matter drop but rather *condemn* his basic values; that is, if he says "My ideals are essentially non-humane", we say "But you *should adopt* humane ideals".[6] The implication, of course, is that our basic values are worthy of his regard, are valid for someone who does not share them. Second, since asserting that our basic values are morally good involves claiming that they possess objective status, we do not need to make a case to that effect—making up our minds that humane ideals are morally good is sufficient and, therefore, a case is superfluous. Third, since we can claim that our basic ideals possess objective status in the absence of a case, the absence of a case holds no threat to our *esprit de corps*—for our *esprit de corps* is threatened only if we must give up claiming that our ideals are worthy of regard from those who do not share them.'

In sum, the above thinkers do not believe that they need to formulate a truth test to validate their basic values; rather, they regard their basic values themselves as analogous to criteria of ethical truth. Therefore, they reject my contention that their 'scepticism' leaves them on a par in terms of justification with an opponent. After all, their own maxims and conduct meet the criteria set by their basic values while those of their opponent do not; and for them, this is sufficient reason to claim that they are superior to him in terms of justification.

Upon reflection, it seems quite natural that these thinkers have interpreted Wittgenstein as they have. Intuitionism has exercized a profound influence over English ethical thought and the resemblance of their position to intuitionism is interesting. I do not mean to say that it *is* intuitionism; for one thing, it certainly rejects the *ontology* of a G. E. Moore, that is, there is no talk of some method of discovering what things possess goodness as a non-natural property. The resemblance is *epistemological*: although he lacked a truth test external to his basic values, the intuitionist felt that he had direct knowledge of what ideals possessed validity; although they lack an external truth test, the above thinkers feel that their commitment to certain ideals as morally good entitles them to claim objective status. Nor do I mean anything so crude as that since intuitionism has been rejected, the position of the above thinkers should be rejected. Rather, by linking it to a venerable philosophical ancestor, I wish to emphasize that it deserves to be taken seriously and argued on its own merits.

*   *   *

The debate which goes on between my own school, the classical school, and thinkers of the above persuasion must certainly be classed as one of the most frustrating in the history of Western philosophy. The first group holds that unless we can make a case that our basic values are worthy of regard from those who do not share them, we have no right to make a claim to that effect; the second holds that a case external to our values is unnecessary, that the fact one really believes that certain distinctive ideals are morally good is sufficient. The two positions are then, diametrically opposed and yet the debate rages on and on, in classrooms and common-rooms, in term papers and journals, without showing any sign of producing a consensus. Indeed, it always seems to end with each side not only certain of the correctness of its position but also exasperated with its opponent, with the 'classicists' saying 'But how can you make such a claim without a case to back it up?' and with the 'modernists' saying 'How can you be so blind to what it means to espouse certain ideals as morally right?' Perhaps if we take a look at the way in which this debate is usually conducted, we can solve the riddle of why each side convinces itself so well while leaving the other side so unmoved. And perhaps we can discover the key to the sort of argument which might break this deadlock. Since the first group endorses the proposition that a case is necessary, I will call its spokesman *pro*; since the second denies that proposition, I will call its representative *contra*. Needless to say, contra is my own creation. No group of philosophers ever banishes dissension from their midst and contra's arguments will represent the views of some much more accurately than others.

Pro (addressing contra): When you encounter someone whose basic values conflict with your own, you claim that your ideals are worthy of regard from him—and then, you deny him the right to claim that his ideals are valid for you. Certainly this means that you must find *something* which *differentiates* you from him. Yet, everything you have said thus far can be just as easily tossed back at you by your opponent. He too can say that the fact he holds certain ideals to be morally good entitles him to claim objective status; he too can condemn your basic values—when you say 'be decent, be humane', he can say 'be tough, be a real competitor'; he too can call his basic values criteria of ethical truth. Indeed, when you do this last, you really add nothing to your argument: to call your basic values criteria of truth is just another way of saying that you have a right to claim objective status even in the absence of a case. All of this leaves you with just one thing which differentiates you from your opponent: the *content* of your ideals differs from his, that is, you hold humane ideals and he holds non-humane ones. But this difference is useless. Here again, if you say 'the fact my ideals differ from yours entitles me to claim objective status', he can answer, 'but the distance between humane and non-humane is just as great from where I stand as from where you do—so why should I not cite this difference and claim that my ideals have objective status?'

Contra (in reply): When you accuse me of denying my opponent the right to claim that his basic values are worthy of my regard, you are not entirely correct. My opponent does have such a right in a sense: he can base his claim to objective status on the same sort of grounds that I do, namely, he believes his basic values to be morally good. But that is the whole point! *He* believes that *his ideals* are morally good *and I do not*—his ideals are not mine, mine are mine. *Given what I believe*, that *my ideals* are morally good, I have all the grounds I need for claiming that my ideals are valid (worthy of regard from those who reject them) and that his are not. Again, from my opponent's perspective, he has the right to claim objective status, but I do not share his perspective. When one asserts the validity of certain ideals, it is legitimate to speak from one's own perspective—from a 'first person' perspective. That is what Wittgenstein meant in saying that when we use moral terms in an absolute sense, we must speak in the first person.[7] And now, we can shed light on another of your mistakes, your belief that the content of ideals is an irrelevant differentiating factor when someone weighs a claim to objective status. For when you imagine two men with conflicting ideals, you treat the difference in content independently of *who* endorses *what content* as morally good. While when I imagine an opponent, I perceive a crucial factor that differentiates me from him— *I accept* humane ideals and *he rejects* them. In other words, if *I* hold certain ideals to be morally good, this creates a situation in which the content of ideals is not irrelevant *for me* in deciding which ones possess objective status. For me, whether or not an ideal *is humane* determines whether or not it has a claim to respect from all mankind.

The trouble with you is that the only differentiating factor you can conceive of (as relevant to claiming objective status) is *a case* external to our basic values, a case which we can make and our opponent cannot. Therefore, all of your arguments are designed to show that I have failed to present such a case, something I have not even attempted to do. You never really come to grips with my principal contention, that a case is *unnecessary*, that the very fact I believe my basic values to be morally good entitles me to claim objective status. And you miss the point of my arguments on behalf of my contention, namely, that the form and usage of moral assessments involve such a claim. Take my argument that we tend to condemn our opponent's basic values. Your response to this is to emphasize that both sides in a dispute can condemn their opponent's values, a rebuttal which is totally beside the point. For I am not both sides in a dispute, I do not condemn both of our ideals. Rather, I espouse mine and condemn his, indeed, often my main reason for condemning my opponent is precisely because of the sort of ideals he holds.

* * *

At this point, the author wishes to come to pro's aid. Contra appears to have done extremely well : he charges that pro's arguments are merely corollaries of pro's main contention (that a case is necessary) and that therefore, they never really touch his own principal contention (that a case is unnecessary). Contra is correct in this. Pro's arguments are essentially circular and that is why contra can evade them so easily. Since pro's arguments are based on pro's main contention, contra need only remind pro that he rejects that contention—need only reiterate his own principal contention time after time. And indeed, contra's reply comes down to little more than such reiteration. However, contra overlooks one important thing : his own arguments suffer from the very same defect he perceives in pro's, that is, his own arguments are also essentially circular. Let me demonstrate this by analysing them.

Contra's first argument attempts to show that the very form of our moral assessments involves a claim to objective status—that when we assert humane ideals to be morally good, we at that very moment claim them to be worthy of regard from all mankind. From this, he concludes that if our moral assessments involve such a claim, no case beyond those assessments is needed to justify such a claim. Now, this conclusion will seem to follow only to someone *already convinced* that a case is unnecessary. For a man who believes a case is necessary will merely say that *if* our moral assessments involve a claim to objective status, we will have to *strip them* of such a claim—unless we can present a case ! This is not to imply that I think contra's analysis of what moral assessments involve is correct. I think moral assessments involve a number of things, universalizability, an assertion that something takes priority over the temptations of desire, but not a claim to objective status. However, for the present, my whole point is that I need not challenge contra's premiss in order to reject his conclusion. Again, even if we do make a claim that our ideals have objective status whenever we assert that they are morally good, the real issue is not whether we do make such a claim but whether we have the right to do so in the absence of a case. Whether we have the right to make such a claim *at all* is crucial; whether the claim is *implied by* our assessments or made *on behalf of* our assessments is trivial. And debate over just what our moral assessments involve merely concerns the latter.

As a counter to this, contra might remind me of my critique of nihilism, that is, my contention that the sceptic (the man who lacks a case) *need not discount* the importance his ideals have for him, need not treat them as if they were of trivial importance for him. And yet, I now say that even if our moral assessments involve a claim to objective status, the absence of a case means we *must discount* them in the sense of stripping them of such a claim. Is there not an inconsistency here? If scepticism does not entail discounting our moral assessments, why strip them of anything, including their claim to objective status? My answer can be simply put: the very factor which allows me to *hold on* to the importance of my ideals *for me* also dictates that *I give up* any claim that my ideals are worthy of regard *from others* (who reject them). The factor referred to is the absence of a case for or test of objective validity: its absence means no one else can show me that his basic values are more worthy of *my regard* than those I hold dear; and its absence means I cannot show others that my basic values are worthy of *their regard* if they happen to loathe them. There is no inconsistency here. For those of us who think a case for objectivity is necessary, my commitment to certain ideals can vouch for their importance to me, but not for their validity for others.

Let the situation of the ethical sceptic be clear. In a word, he can take his ideals *seriously*. He can cherish them, praise them, live by them, fight for them, etc.; he can use them to condemn his opponents—condemn them lock, stock, and barrel, that is, condemn not only their actions but everything about them from their most specific precepts to their basic values. However, when the sceptic praises his ideals and issues his condemnations, he must be willing to grant that they are worthy of regard only from himself and his partisans—he cannot claim objective status. It may be objected that taking our ideals seriously *means* holding that they are worthy of regard from all men including our opponents. But the reader now knows what I would say to this, namely: even if that is so, in the absence of a case, *how* seriously do we have *a right* to take our moral assessments? This is not to deny that since I take my ideals seriously, I will find it important to be able to claim objective status. But again, my commitment can only make such a claim terribly important to me; it cannot vouch for the claim itself.

Contra's second argument seizes upon the concession I made above, that the absence of a case does not prevent us from condemning our opponent's values, *including his basic values*. Contra emphasizes that where moral matters are concerned, we do not allow an opponent's refusal to concur in our condemnation of his acts to go unchallenged; when he bases his refusal on his differing basic values (e.g. non-humane ones), we go on to condemn those values. This argument, like contra's first, is likely to convince only the already converted; for those who believe a case is needed, it merely poses the question of the status of our *second condemnation*. True, we have challenged the thing (his basic values) on which our opponent bases his refusal to concur; but in the absence of a case on behalf of our challenge, what right have we to claim that *it* is worthy of his regard? Certainly our opponent is going to refuse to concur in our condemnation of his values just as strongly as he refused to concur in our original condemnation of his acts. In other words, for our second condemnation to render our first condemnation worthy of our opponent's regard, *it itself* would have to be worthy of his regard. And if contra resorts to the same method to bolster our second condemnation that he used to bolster our first, he is caught in an endless regression. The sequence would run : I condemn your acts ; I condemn the basic values on which you base your refusal to concur in the above condemnation ; I condemn your refusal to concur in my condemnation of your basic values ; I condemn the basic values on which you base your refusal to concur in the above condemnation ; and so on *ad infinitum*. All in all, the author sees nothing particularly impressive about praising or condemning *basic values* as distinct from *acts*—unless we can present a case on behalf of our own basic values and against those we condemn.

Once again, contra may counterattack, this time by asking : 'Why do you place so much emphasis on justifying our basic values, on a case *external* to our value system? Note that the sceptic is not barred from offering a certain sort of justification. He can justify his subordinate value assessments (e.g. his condemnation of capital punishment) in terms of his basic values (e.g. humane ones) ; that is, he can offer a case *internal* to his value system on behalf of his ideals. And when you say that he must not stop there but must go on to justify his basic values, must cite some sort of test of ethical truth, are not you yourself caught in an endless regression? For why should we let you stop there, why not demand that you justify your truth test in terms of some more fundamental criterion and so on *ad infinitum*? After all, *justification must stop somewhere*, so why not with our basic values?' In reply, it makes all the difference in the world whether justification stops at or goes beyond our basic values. The first allows for no more than a purely *partisan* justification, a case which depends on the *acceptance* of a certain set of basic values for its force ; the second holds out the hope of a *non-partisan* justification, a case which shows that our ideals are worthy of regard even from those who *do not accept* our basic values. Moreover, we are not driven to extend the process of justification beyond a non-partisan

4

truth test. Such a test gives us what we want, namely, a solution to the problem of how to justify our ideals when faced with an ideological opponent whose basic values conflict with our own; therefore, no further levels of justification are needed! It may not give us *all* we want, of course; as we shall see, it may give us a case in terms of one form of goodness and not another. However, such a limitation leads us to desire a similar case, *a non-partisan case*, in terms of that other form. It does not engender a need for a case beyond a non-partisan case.

I wish to emphasize that up to now I have merely been driving home my point that contra's arguments are just as circular as pro's. They gain their force only by way of an implicit or unstated assumption of the truth of contra's main contention (that a case is unnecessary); none of them argue towards that proposition by way of a direct attack upon pro's main contention (that a case is necessary). Therefore, pro can evade them by the simple expedient of reiterating his principal contention. My arguments thus far constitute an attempt to teach pro how to do this—I am *quite aware* that they amount to little more than constant reiteration of his principal contention.

In other words, I have *not yet* tried to convert contra; rather, I have tried to solve the problem of why the debate between pro and contra is so indecisive. Circularity is part of the answer; but why does each participant fail to see that it has infected *him*? My explanation is this: each side is so convinced of the truth of its position that it assumes that *the burden of proof rests on its opponent*. Once you make that assumption, you do not feel that you need mount a direct assault on his main contention—working out the corollaries to your position seems sufficient. And once you make that assumption, your opponent's failure to come to grips with your main contention is seen as pure evasion. In effect, your circularity seems only appropriate; his circularity seems fatal to his cause. The result is a debate in which each side is *satisfied* to define the other out of existence, a debate which never rises above 'Since a case is necessary (or unnecessary), what he says is beside the point'. Like ships in the night, arguments slip past one another without ever making direct contact. However, from solving the above problem, we have also discovered the key to another, namely, the sort of argument which might break this philosophical deadlock. We must find a way of directly attacking contra's principal contention; and ideally, our arguments would be based on something pro and contra have in common.

*   *   *

Let us, then, begin our attack by concentrating on the real issue which separates pro and contra: when claiming our ideals are worthy of regard by all men, must we take the fact that others have differing basic values into account (and therefore, make a case); or can we confine ourselves to our own evaluations—hold that the fact we find our ideals to be morally good is sufficient (and therefore, no case is needed)? Now, the latter contention poses the question of whether it is reasonable to claim that our ideals are worthy of regard *by others* without taking the *values of others* into account. After all, I am not talking to myself in ideological debate—I am *addressing someone*—my audience consists of all mankind. Can we just treat our audience as ciphers, ignore the fact that many of them do not possess our basic values? And if we acknowledge that fact, certainly we must grant that given their basic values, it makes no sense for them to share our regard for the ideals we recommend. Indeed, at times, contra seems tacitly to accept this last. The very fact that when faced by opponents with conflicting basic values he felt he had to condemn those values is significant—it constitutes a tacit admission that *given their basic values*, there was *no reason* for them to accept his recommendations about how to live. And if contra feels obliged to take the values of his opponents into account when recommending acts, why not when claiming that they should espouse his basic values?

Contra would no doubt reply to this initial attack much as he did to pro's arguments: 'Of course, I grant that *given* my opponent's basic values, it makes sense for him to reject my recommendations. I am quite aware that I often face men with conflicting values and that this poses serious problems, e.g. the practical problem of how to win them over. But my main point is this: I refuse to accept my opponent's basic values *as given*; I insist on evaluating them. To be explicit, I do take my opponent's values into account for a number of reasons. However, when deciding what ideals are worthy of regard from all mankind (including him), I take his evaluations into account only *as data*, as something to be assessed by me; I do not take them into account *as evaluations*, as something to be taken at face-value. Which is to say that when deciding what ideals are worthy of regard, I restrict myself to my own evaluations, to a first person perspective; but this is perfectly legitimate, as I have said before and as Wittgenstein said before me.'

But, to resume the attack, even if one restricts oneself to one's own evaluations, does this really solve the problem of what ideals are worthy of regard? When I enter into my own universe of value, what if I find not unity but conflict? For example, I may discover that at times, I give as my ultimate justification of an act a humane criterion and that at other times, I cite a criterion of personal revenge—and further, that both of these criteria mean a great deal to me. In a word, what if I find that I am genuinely divided between opposing sets of basic values? In that event, I am not only unable to recommend certain ideals as worthy of regard from all mankind, I am not even able to decide which ideals *I* should take seriously. This remains true, of course, only so long as I remain divided. But this brings me to my real point: in the absence of an external test, *how* do I go about *achieving unity*? In the absence of an external test, I am thrown entirely on my personal resources, which is to say I am left asking questions like: which set of values or ideals stirs me most; or given two men, one who lives by ideals A and the other by ideals B, which do I admire most; or which values am I most willing to use to pattern my life; or which do I wish to hand on to my children? The important thing about all of these questions is that they will lead me to choose the humane values *only if* those values possess a *stronger hold over me* than the ethic of revenge. Which means that if another man follows my method of resolving my conflict, and if his make-up is such that revenge holds more sway over him than a humane ethic, he will opt for non-humane values! In other words, the sceptic, the man who eschews an external test, cannot recommend *his own method* of ending a genuine division in his basic values to others *if* he wishes to tell them that *his own ideals* are worthy of their regard. Having achieved a unity in favour of humane values, he can of course go to others and say: 'Choose my basic values, the values I have ended up with—resolve your struggle in favour of humane ideals.' But this invites the crushing retort: 'That is not how *you* resolved *your* struggle! You did not just copy someone else's ideals. You followed the precept of "know thyself"—you tried to find out what ideals really held you in their grasp.'

This seems to me the supreme dilemma of contra's position, the position of those who (unlike most sceptics) believe they can go on claiming that their ideals are worthy of regard from all men despite the absence of an external truth test. If they have ever been torn by that terrible chaos which signals a genuine conflict of basic values, they must say to others: either, follow my ideals but not my method of resolving your agony; or, follow my method but *I cannot tell you which ideals to elect*. Note this last phrase carefully. For the real dilemma contra faces is not that his method may not give the palm to *his* ideals. If we espouse a test of ethical truth, our own ideals may be found wanting *vis-à-vis* other ideals; but at least those other ideals are now seen to be worthy of regard. The real dilemma contra faces is that if his method of resolving conflicts is applied, *no* set of ideals emerges as worthy of regard by mankind. Therefore, how can he claim, in the absence of an external test, that certain basic values are worthy of regard by all? And his right to make that claim constitutes the very soul of his position.

It may be objected that I have been unfair to contra. Even if the lack of an external test throws me back entirely on my own personal resources, might I not use some more complex method of resolving a conflict in my basic values than those described above? No doubt, for the above description is not offered as a complete account of the alternatives available to the sceptic; it is offered to make an epistemological point. Perhaps the best way to make that point is to say this: come forward with your more elaborate method. And if it seems to extricate you from your dilemma, I will wager that one of two things has happened. *Either*, you are not imagining yourself *genuinely* divided between conflicting basic values; rather, you have evaded the problem by assuming you are basically committed to one set (e.g. humane values) and are merely mopping up on peripheral (and non-humane) commitments, saying to yourself something like 'Since that maxim is cruel, I must purge myself of it'. *Or*, you are groping your way towards a non-partisan test!—towards a test which bears a suspicious resemblance to one of the classical tests of objective status in ethics, be it Platonic or Aristotelian, Kantian or Utilitarian. And on this wager, I will rest my case.

I believe that the above argument is sufficient to undermine contra's position. However, I wish to add a second which stands or falls independently of the first. Let us go back to the man who has achieved unity in his basic values. If I am such a man, and if I restrict myself to my own evaluations, I thereby do enter a universe of evaluation in which there is *no dispute* about what ideals are worthy of regard. But what is the significance of this? Does the fact an ideal is dominant make it any more than an ideal held in regard *without opposition*—does it convert it into an ideal worthy of regard even from *those who oppose it*? In other words, contra's position seems to me akin to the argument from unanimity, albeit he bases his claims on a 'unanimity of one'. Both focus on an evaluative universe in which an ideal is *held to be* worthy of regard and then claim that it *is* worthy of regard. When the advocates of the argument from unanimity do this, when they tell us that certain ideals are held (or more often, will soon be held) by all mankind, I am unimpressed. I always say: 'What if some historical event, such as a nuclear explosion which kills off everyone but a few groups of Nazis, gives us a human race unanimously dedicated to non-humane ideals? Would this mean that those ideals were worthy of regard?' And I am similarly unimpressed by the fact that events of my personal history, such as strong and dedicated parents, or mutually reinforcing peer groups, have created an individual undivided (I hope) in his allegiance to humanism. Not that I am resting my case on an extreme environmentalism: if the Nazis triumphed by their own efforts, this would make no difference; and, as the reader already knows, if I had battled my own way to a coherent humanism, my point would be the same. It is this: lack of opposition within a universe of evaluation, whether that universe involves all men or only one, is a bad basis for the right of certain ideals to be held in regard. Therefore, I reject both the argument from unanimity and contra's position. And my hope is that pro and contra can find some common ground here so as to resolve their debate. After all, both sides in this debate often cite the argument from unanimity as a paradigm of a bad argument in ethics.

William James stands as an example of a philosopher of the first rank who carefully considered just what claims we have a right to make on the basis of our own evaluations. James imagines a universe containing a single man and tells us that what that man holds to be good is absolutely good, but *only* in the sense that he is the sole judge of good and evil who exists, only because 'he inhabits a moral solitude'.[8] It is not a matter of such a man having the right to claim objective status, that his ideals are worthy of regard from those who do not share them. It is just a matter of his being in a universe of evaluation which *does not pose* the question of ethical truth, for *no one exists* who does not share his basic values.[9] James drives his point home by adding a second man to his universe. He gives his two men the option of each refusing to take the evaluations of the other into account.[10] But he denies them the right to use this option as the basis of a claim that one's own ideals are worthy of regard from one's companion. Indeed, James anticipates contra's very position! He poses the question of whether a particular consciousness can make an ideal right (obligatory on others) by feeling it to be right.[11] He even puts the question *in the first person*, 'Shall we then simply proclaim our ideals as the law-giving ones?', and answers with an emphatic 'No'.[12] He even holds that God Himself has no right to claim that what He believes to be morally good is worthy of regard by others![13]

Unfortunately, James does not spell out his reasons for his stand. But his contention that by confining ourselves to our own evaluations we merely *avoid posing* the problem of ethical truth contains the germ of my second argument. We must not use the conditions under which a problem *does not arise* (when mankind happens to be unanimous— or when I confine myself to my own evaluations and find unity) to argue that no solution is needed when that problem *does arise* (when mankind is divided—or when I wish to claim my ideals are valid for those who do not share them). And incidentally, we must not confuse the conditions under which a problem does not arise (unity) with a solution to that problem (a case for validity despite disunity). Further, while I do not presume to commit James to my first argument, I find the following of great interest: James imagines a man with conflicting values attempting to achieve unity despite the absence of an external truth test ('Truth supposes a standard outside of the thinker . . .'); and he assumes that such a man is thrown back on his own personal resources, that he can do no more than attempt to discover whether certain values have a stronger hold over him than others.[14]

Well, then, I side with James. Whether I achieve unity or remain torn, restricting myself to my own evaluations does not provide an adequate basis for claiming objective status. My own unity *is* an adequate foundation for universalizing my ideals. However, as we have seen, universalizability is not equivalent to objective status—perhaps some failure to distinguish these two engenders confusion on this question?

This concludes my attempt to attack directly contra's principal contention. My arguments seem sound to me; however, at times, I despair of their effectiveness. Contra's position has become received opinion in certain quarters; and the reluctance to abandon his position is so understandable—we all know dedicated men who tend to feel that their basic values just must be worthy of regard from others, despite their inability to show that this is so. Further, pro and contra have become adept at defining one another's arguments out of existence and my attacking arguments may well suffer a similar fate. Therefore, as this section closes, I wish to remind the reader of my thesis that the debate between pro and contra has been a stand-off up to now, a thesis of whose truth I am fully convinced. For certainly, *even if* those of you who share contra's position discount my attacking arguments, this thesis *in itself* should give you a severe jolt. At the very least, it should make you understand why 'classicists' like myself are as stubborn about giving up our position as you are about giving up yours— and convince you to abandon the notion (as I have) that the burden of proof rests on your opponent. And if that happens, my attacking arguments may come into their own. They may awaken doubts and encourage those who share contra's position to reflect carefully before they answer the following question: do you *really believe* that just making up your mind about what is morally good gives you the right to claim that your conclusions are worthy of regard from all mankind?

*   *   *

Our refutation of contra's position has brought us a bonus, that is, we can now pin-point precisely what it is about ethical scepticism which threatens our *esprit de corps*. If my refutation is sound, the *logical* consequence of scepticism is that we do not have the right to claim that our ideals are worthy of regard from those who do not share them, something that most sceptics recognize (contra is an exception, of course). Loss of *esprit de corps* is a *psychological* consequence of scepticism whose degree is a function of how strongly one *wants* to make the above claim. Clearly men like contra and myself want very much to do so—and therefore, if both of us became sceptics and both of us faced up to the logical consequences of scepticism, our sense of loss and frustration would be very great. Clearly Wittgenstein wanted very much to do so—recall his expressions, so deeply felt, of regard for those who wish to use value terms in an absolute sense.

Since the psychological consequences of scepticism are fundamentally a reaction to its logical consequences, let us make the latter a bit more explicit. If the sceptic is correct, we cannot claim that our ideals are worthy of regard from anyone except ourselves and our partisans, those who already share our basic values. Which means that the real significance of ethical scepticism comes down to this : any *ideological appeals* we issue on behalf of our way of life, any claims we make that it is best for mankind, must be regarded as having either purely *partisan* or *rhetorical* significance. If the sceptic is right, we can sing the praises of the way of life we champion for the benefit of our fellow partisans, perhaps in order to raise their spirits. And we can hope thereby to have a favourable rhetorical effect on those whose values differ from our own, that is, we can hope that they will focus on our attractive phrases rather than on what they might find unattractive about our way of life. But this is to say that we can do little more than hold up our ideals for partisan admiration. In a word, scepticism reduces the status of our appeals to something analogous to that of a *battle-cry*. A battle-cry can arouse one's troops ; and it can even stir the emotions of onlookers who do not really share one's cause, for after all, the sight of troops marching in support of a cause has a certain attraction in itself—'all of man's reason flies before a drum'.

Now we can understand why the psychological reaction of so many men to ethical scepticism is so strong : for many deeply committed men, battle-cries are not enough. When faced with a loathed ideological opponent, they want to be able to do more than hold up their basic ideals for partisan admiration. For any partisan, humane or not, can shout battle-cries. They want to be able to say more on behalf of their ideals than an opponent can say for his, to be able to say that their ideals have non-partisan validity, that theirs are worthy of respect from mankind in a way in which his are not. Those who have felt the helplessness of this situation, the prolonged tight-clenched agony, will not soon forget it. And indeed, it seems to me that the *humane* man feels a special sort of agony when confronted with scepticism in that the peculiar *content* of his ideals makes him sensitive to their *status*. A humane man *cares* about what is good for each and every human being in a way in which a Social Darwinist or Nietzschean does not. Thus, his inability to claim that his ideals are worthy of regard from mankind, except in partisan terms, can be particularly demoralizing. To bring this point home, imagine that you and your ideological opponent are debating before an audience not yet fully committed to either humane or non-humane ideals, an audience whose values leave them evenly balanced. What pain to admit that you can say no more to them than your opponent can, namely : 'In so far as you are *already with me*, my ideals are valid for you ; but in so far as you are *against me*, they are not.'

I want to stress that it is *because* certain men are dedicated to their ideals that they suffer when they become sceptics. This may avoid some misconceptions about my use of the word 'rhetorical'. When I say that the ideological appeals a sceptic makes on behalf of his ideals have only rhetorical significance, I do not mean that he is shallow or insincere or issues appeals merely to chatter or titillate—that his appeals are rhetorical in that sense. I mean that his appeals are rhetorical in this sense : he cannot claim that they are worthy of regard from *those to whom they are directed*. After all, his ideological appeals hold up a certain way of life for the edification of mankind ; and yet, he cannot claim that they are worthy of regard from mankind, at least that portion of mankind which needs converting. His appeals are valid for himself and his fellow partisans, of course ; but that means they are worthy of regard primarily from *those who issue them*! And again, it is precisely because he takes his ideals so seriously that he finds this situation so demoralizing.

Philosophers who grant that ethical scepticism poses a real problem often add that it cannot be important for very many people. They point to the fact that one needs a certain amount of sophistication to comprehend the problem and argue that therefore, however significant it may seem to philosophers, it can hardly mean much to the man in the street. I am not going to be so rash as to speculate about the 'man in the street', but I do know something first-hand of the political agitator in the street, at least in an American context. And I am convinced that many of America's best young people, many of those agitating and fighting and dying in the struggle for social justice, *do* worry about this problem. They feel terribly threatened by the thought of their humane ideals standing mute before a non-humane opponent.

I do not deny that most of those of whom I speak lack a sophisticated grasp of the problem of scepticism ; but their very over-simplification of the issue renders it *even more* emotionally explosive. For the current crop of agitators, the issue often *is* a case of eternal ethical truths versus matters of taste. And there is no evidence that over-simplification of the problem by a previous generation of reformers dampened its significance for them ; a look at the bitterness of the debate between the absolutists and relativists in the Jeffersonian camp prior to World War I may convince us that quite the contrary was true. Further, to an unprecedented degree, political agitators today are men with a university education ; to increase their sophistication concerning the problem of scepticism and to offer them a solution of sorts seems to me both possible and important.

Those philosophers who refuse to grant that our problem has any real significance tend to save a certain argument, the one they find most convincing perhaps, to last. They argue as follows: 'If we are really dealing with a dispute that involves *basic* values and if the disputants' values *really* conflict, how could we resolve such a dispute? Facts cannot resolve it because they are irrelevant to conflicts of basic values; values cannot resolve it precisely because the disputants have conflicting values. Thus, the resolution of such a dispute is seen to be *logically impossible*. And how can anyone get emotionally upset over being unable to do something that is logically impossible? This is as insane as brooding over one's inability to draw a square circle.'

In reply, first, it is by no means obvious that men (even sane ones) cannot agonize over something that is logically impossible. If we abandon geometrical examples, like a square circle, for theological ones, things look somewhat different. For example, Jean-Paul Sartre believes that the concept of God, as non-contingent existence, is logically self-contradictory. If a religious man decided that Sartre was correct in this, it is doubtful that he would fail to agonize— that he would throw up his hands and say 'how foolish to be concerned about the logically impossible'. Second, and more important, I feel that I can deal with the above argument, not so much by refuting it as by showing that it is beside the point, at least as far as *ideological* disputes are concerned—and at least as far as my sort of '*half-solution*' (to the problem of scepticism) is concerned. In effect, I hope to show that it does not bar an appeal to evidence, evidence relevant to three empirical hypotheses. The reader will have to wait for my argument but if it is correct, then even if the evidence favours the sceptic, at least we will have permission to weep. For certainly, one can be upset when factual hypotheses that one wishes very much to be true are falsified.

In closing, let me emphasize that the extent to which

different men agonize over ethical scepticism *does* come down to a matter of psychology. Some men have reacted with horror to the death of God, others have not. Probably it is enough for some men to be humane partisans, although I am not in their number. But to be told that the only reason *anyone* is concerned about the threat to objectivity in ethics is because of muddled thinking—that is too much. Those who are concerned see what is involved only too well.

NOTES

[1] Ludwig Wittgenstein, 'A Lecture on Ethics', *Philosophical Review*, January 1965, p. 5.

[2] *Ibid.*, pp. 5, 7.

[3] *Ibid.*, p. 7.

[4] Rush Rhees, 'Some Developments in Wittgenstein's View of Ethics', *Philosophical Review*, January 1965, pp. 17, 20.

[5] Wittgenstein, *op. cit.*, p. 12; Friedrich Waismann, 'Notes on Talks with Wittgenstein', *Philosophical Review*, January 1965, p. 16.

[6] Wittgenstein, *op. cit.*, p. 5.

[7] Waismann, *op. cit.*, p. 16.

[8] William James, *The Will to Believe and Other Essays in Popular Philosophy* (New York: Longmans, Green, and Co., 1897), pp. 190–1.

[9] *Ibid.*, p. 191.

[10] *Ibid.*, pp. 191–2.

[11] *Ibid.*, p. 193.

[12] *Ibid.*, p. 199.

[13] *Ibid.*, pp. 193–4.

[14] *Ibid.*, p. 191.

3

Jefferson and James

If humane men with strong ethical and political commitments *ought* to feel that the problem of ethical scepticism is
significant, then we should be able to point to cases where
such men *were* concerned about this problem. And we can :
the American social and political scene furnishes us with
some excellent examples. Indeed, the issue of ethical
absolutism versus relativism engendered a heated debate
among American reformers at the turn of the century, a
debate that has never been concluded.

America is worth our attention on other grounds. Many
U.S. thinkers, while granting that the above problem is
significant, would argue that my own adverse reaction to
the challenge of ethical scepticism is wholly inappropriate.
They hold that value scepticism is to be welcomed, and
welcomed for more reasons than one. First, they assert that
belief in the doctrine of ethical relativism encourages men
in fact to be friends of humane ideals. It is not at all un-
common to find a historian in America telling us that his
period teaches this lesson : that the best safeguard of the
tolerance which is the soul of both humane conduct and
political freedom is a rejection by men of ethical absolutes
and an espousal of relativism. Second, they assert that
ethical scepticism can best provide a *philosophical base* for
humane ideals. This is an argument that to my knowledge
first appears in American thought in the essays of William
James. James holds that we can best provide a justification
for humane ethics by doing two things : granting the sceptic

what he thinks to be a crucial concession, that one cannot make a valid case for objectivity in ethics ; and then, using that very concession to argue in favour of humane ethics, humane ethics of a sort that finds realization in an open society with a civil libertarian political system.

Why did Jeffersonians in America develop such an acute concern about the problem of ethical scepticism ? What led some of their number to embrace scepticism as a friend ? My attempt to answer these questions entails a brief excursion into the history of political thought in nineteenth-century America. However, before I begin, I wish to make one thing clear : when these men speak of scepticism, they do not refer to something like contra's position—we have left contra behind. The more sophisticated refer to the thorough-going (and logically coherent) scepticism of those who deny our right to claim objective status ; and the more naïve, as always, think in terms of eternal ethical truths versus matters of taste.

*   *   *

The century opens with the triumph of Jefferson over the Federalists in the election of 1800 and with the triumph of the Jeffersonian ideal. There emerges a national consensus about political ideals and their ethical base and while the ethical base is soon shattered, the Jeffersonian ideal has persisted in America, at least in broad outline, right down to the present day. Note that I am giving the Jeffersonian ideal a very broad construction, one that renders it identical with what has remained constant in America's dominant political consensus. Let me, then, clarify what I mean by the Jeffersonian ideal and describe the ethical base upon which it originally rested. This will also afford the reader a rough description of the sort of life that I think best for mankind.

The Jeffersonian ideal is descended from the humanist ideal of the Enlightenment, an ideal which of course transcends the American context. Humanism holds up a certain way of life as best for man, a life characterized by humane activity and comradeship, fulfilling work, leisure brightened by artistic or scientific or athletic pursuits, and a balance in favour of spontaneity over coercion. As a short-hand description of the humanist ideal, I usually use the phrase 'a life of humane love and creative work'.

There is a danger in this phrase in that it could be misleading as to what the humanist ideal means in practice. It would really be better to call this ideal a life *oriented* towards humane love and creative work, so as to indicate that while the features described above are characteristic of a humanistic way of life, they are not meant to provide a full description of *any* actual way of life. Any full-blooded way of life involves a range of values and activities of tremendous complexity. Describing an actual humanistic society in terms of humane love and creative work could easily give the impression that people just go about being humane and creative and never drink, gamble, waste time in delightful ways, engage in social rituals, etc. Another trap concerning phrasing : the fact that I am dealing with mostly quite anti-humane opponents in this work often leads me to describe the humanist ideal as 'the humane life'. But this should not be taken literally, as implying that those who live the life that suits man best are *perfectly* humane. Actually, of course, they would suffer severely if they had to be perfectly humane and never enjoyed a touch of malicious gossip, exciting rivalries, a variety of small triumphs, etc.

Thanks to the Jeffersonians, the humanist ideal was elaborated in America in a way that gave it a strong civil libertarian emphasis and thus, my short-hand for the Jeffersonian ideal will be 'the humane-libertarian way of life'. This ideal has two facets and, following Erich Fromm, we might best describe it in terms of freedom *from* and freedom *to*. It emphasizes affording men freedom from exploitation by government and private wealth, freedom from being used as means for the ends of the powerful, so that each man may enjoy freedom to develop his mind, character, talents, and capacity for human relationships. In twentieth-century America, this ideal evolved, at least in the

5

hands of left-wing Jeffersonians, so as to include an emphasis on the need for certain *social conditions* if the individual's freedom was to have any substance. These Jeffersonians went beyond rights such as political and religious freedom to speak of the right of Americans to full employment, decent working conditions, an adequate standard of living, social security, education and cultural opportunities, etc.

It is useful, in defining the Jeffersonian ideal, to contrast it with its chief challenger for the allegiance of Americans, a challenger that has always threatened its dominance and which, particularly since the rise of the robber barons after the civil war, has enjoyed more than one decade of temporary victory. We will call this other ideal the competitive-individualistic ideal. It has a vulgarized Nietzschean streak, that is, it tends to glorify power and success, particularly in the economic arena. Its emphasis is on leaving men free from all restraints except the rules of a certain game, a game that maximizes a man's freedom to compete for the prizes of wealth, power, and social status. Its Nietzschean tendencies encourage a lack of emphasis on humane activity on behalf of the unfortunate, that is, little sympathy is 'wasted' on the losers in the struggle for power and wealth. It should be noted, by the way, that this ideal and the Jeffersonian ideal have their similarities as well as their differences. Many Jeffersonians, particularly right-wing Jeffersonians, have aimed primarily not at eliminating or humanizing competition but merely at making sure that all competitors start on an equal footing. Indeed, it is precisely these similarities that have made the holders of these two ideals such deadly rivals, have rendered each capable of winning over converts from among those in the other's camp.

Originally, America developed not only a rough consensus about political ideals but also a real consensus about ethical truth. I refer, of course, to the doctrine of modern natural right. Following Locke, the early Jeffersonians held that men were God's creations and therefore were not to be exploited or destroyed; further, they held that nature had made men free and had favoured no man with a divine sceptre that entitled him to rule over others. This was taken to provide an ethical base for both humanism and political freedom, to establish that men were precious and had a right to be governed by their own consent. Government in turn was obliged to respect man's natural rights, rights such as freedom of thought, expression, etc. The doctrine of natural right not only captured the allegiance of the intellectuals but also filtered down to the grass roots. At the time of the state constitutional conventions, we find the citizens of county after county telling their delegates, in effect, not to come home if they barter away any of their constituents' natural rights.[1] The ageing Jefferson took great satisfaction in the fact that his fellow Americans continued to share his reverence for the ethical foundations of the Republic's political ideals. In 1824, two years before his death, Jefferson wrote: 'Nothing then is unchangeable but the inherent and unalienable rights of man!'[2]

Without exerting himself in the least, Darwin battered the unchangeable rights of man into a shambles. Americans did not have time to do much with Darwin until the Civil War was over. However, when they did find time, they did their worst.

After the Civil War, the nation began to industrialize in earnest and most Americans were caught up in a craze to exploit the resources of the continent. Envy and admiration for the captain of industry was so common that the Jeffersonian ideal came near to being submerged by the competitive-individualistic ideal of the robber barons. Those who favoured the latter were not slow to use Darwin to justify the power and status of the industrial rich. The cut-throat competition for wealth of the robber barons was held to be the social equivalent of the biological struggle for survival. This implied that existing social institutions and their élites were the fit that had survived the evolutionary struggle and therefore, represented the highest level of social progress ever attained. Those who clung to the Jeffersonian ideal reacted strongly against this sort of conservative Social Darwinism. They were thoroughly alarmed by the excesses of the industrial rich and by the rising power of the trusts. While left- and right-wing Jeffersonians might disagree about how to deal with these new problems, none of them were willing to concede that the corporate élite represented the highest level of social progress ever attained. As Eric Goldman points out, they felt the need for an ideology that would break 'the steel chain of ideas' which lent dignity to the status of the industrial rich. They found their ideology in reform Darwinism.[3]

The reform Darwinists emphasized the environmental side of Darwin's theory, the fact that the changing environment was the crucial factor in prompting new evolutionary developments. They held that this applied to man in society and that, therefore, man could change and progress only if his social environment altered. As for the conservative Social Darwinists, they were guilty of the crime of crimes, of being pre-Darwinian. For they wanted to *freeze* man's socio-economic environment, to maintain the socio-economic system of late nineteenth-century America forever intact. And the reform Darwinists went further; they used their environmentalism as a weapon against all those social scientists who claimed that their particular discipline confirmed the truth of conservative Social Darwinism. They elaborated a blanket critique in two steps: first, they held that the views a man had about ethics, politics, economics, evolution, etc., were nothing but a reflection of his socio-economic environment; second, they held that if a man's views were relative to his social environment, they were also relative in regard to truth, that is, they equated *sociological* relativism with *philosophical* relativism. Of course, this sort of critique pleased the reform Darwinists greatly. They could lump together all of the social science that bolstered the *status quo, laissez-faire* economics, Westermarckian anthropology, Spencerian sociology, legalistic jurisprudence, etc., and dismiss it as nothing more than a rationalization that served to protect the privileged status of an economic élite.[4]

However, sooner or later someone was bound to point out that this weapon was a double-edged sword. If every man's views were purely a social product, and if sociological relativism equalled truth relativism, what about the ethics, politics, economics, etc., of the Jeffersonians? They too must be only relative. One of the first to appreciate this was Thorstein Veblen in 1899. Apparently Veblen could accept value relativism, could accept the fact that his basic values were no more objective than those of his opponents.[5] On the other hand, scholars such as Charles Beard later on became deeply disturbed by the problem of relativism. Goldman quotes Beard as saying that 'the apostle of relativity is destined to be destroyed by the child of his own brain'.[6]

Others reacted to this child of environmentalism on a practical, rather than a philosophical, level. By 1913, Walter Lippmann was convinced that reformers should greet thorough-going ethical relativism with jubilation.[7] He said that any belief in an 'intrinsic good' would eventually be used to serve the cause of reaction and bolster the *status quo*. Lippmann later altered his views[8] and, even at the time, there were those who doubted that relativism would in fact make friends for the reformer's ideals. Herbert Croly whose 'new nationalism' was to base reform on an ethic of dedication to the national welfare was horrified. Harold Stearns in his *Liberalism in America* launched a savage attack on relativism and pragmatism as fatal to the *esprit de corps* of American reform.[9] Indeed, many reformers were uneasy, particularly since they tended to over-simplify the problems posed by ethical relativism. To them, it seemed to make the excesses of the robber barons permissible; it seemed to make the humane foundations of the Jeffersonian ideal merely a matter of taste. But none of these thinkers, including Beard, Croly, Stearns, etc., had much philosophical skill and thus, none of them could offer a convincing defence of ethical truth.

By way of contrast, William James, a philosopher of the first rank, thought on a much higher plane than any of the above. In 1891, before they were aware of the problem of ethical relativism and, as we will see later, before they had managed to botch the formulation of the problem, he had attempted a solution.[10] James did not feel that he could refute relativism directly. He felt that he both must and should make the concession that the sceptic demanded, namely, that it was impossible to defend objectivity in ethics. But what if he could show that this concession was not a *crucial* concession? What if he could show that this concession made possible a powerful justification of humane ethics, that it set the stage for a condemnation of the robber barons? He would then have passed between the horns of the whole dilemma.

But even this does not exhaust the profound significance of what James tried to do. If he could prove his point, he would not only have found a neat escape from a philosophical dilemma. He would not only have chalked up a few points against the robber barons. He would have provided the basis for a *new national consensus*! If he could only show that granting the ethical sceptic his crucial concession actually allowed one to defend the humane-libertarian ideal, he could unite all of the bickering Jeffersonians in a higher synthesis. Those who proclaimed ethical relativism a friend of their ideals would feel vindicated. Those who feared that relativism would undermine the status of humane values and sap the élan of their cohorts would rejoice to find their fears routed. For the first time since Jefferson, since the fall of the doctrine of natural right, the nation could unite and with one voice acclaim James's position as the ethical basis of its political ideal.

*   *   *

The brevity of this historical sketch has rendered it superficial, but its aim is quite a modest one. It is an attempt to isolate a single thread, slender but significant, that is entwined in the history of ideas of nineteenth-century America. At the beginning of the century, there exists a real consensus which bases the Jeffersonian ideal upon a certain brand of ethical truth, namely, the doctrine of modern natural right. By the close of the century, significant thinkers are arguing along these lines: that *rejection* of ethical truth can best provide a *philosophical* base for the Jeffersonian ideal; and that this humane-libertarian ideal finds its best friends *in fact* among those who espouse ethical relativism. We can now go on to make a critical analysis of these two assertions; let us examine the second assertion first.

U.S. intellectuals exist, particularly in the ranks of the historians, who derive considerable satisfaction from a certain method of arguing about whether the adherents of ethical absolutism or relativism prove to be the best friends of humane-libertarian ideals. Their method is that of Cephalus in Plato's *Republic*. They do not deign to give their readers general definitions that would disclose what they believe distinguishes the doctrine of ethical scepticism from belief in ethical truth. Rather, they pick their particular period and then turn to the device of definition by enumeration, that is to say, they 'clarify' the above by holding up certain historical figures as examples of what it means to believe in one or the other. The historian who thinks he believes in absolutes usually holds up the more craven and unscrupulous figures of his era as examples of how relativism breeds compromise. Radical intellectuals who rationalized the crimes of Stalin or liberal New Dealers who felt no indignation about graft often head the list. The historian who has a preference for relativism is likely to do something similar, that is, he trots out the most loathsome of the fanatics of his period as examples of what absolutes can do to a man. He can be counted on to cite the prohibitionists, the more bizarre suffragettes, with perhaps the Grand Dragon of the Klu-Klux-Klan thrown in for good measure. It is *de rigueur* to close out such a passage with the solemn warning that 'he who aims at heaven on earth only succeeds in creating hell' or something equally terrifying.

It is, then, easy to show that either ethical relativism or absolutism hurts the cause of humane-libertarian ideals if you *define* what it means to believe in them by listing either cowards or lunatics. Naturally, the better historians do not operate on this level. Hofstadter, for example, in his *The Age of Reform* deals with the question in a much more balanced fashion. Hofstadter feels that Goldman over-emphasizes the extent to which relativism created problems for American reform, that is, he feels that American reform has been victimized far more by a form of ethical absolut-ism.[11] However, he does not set up a straw man. He lists examples of men led astray by both relativism and absolutism. More important, he does not talk about the deleterious effects upon tolerance and humane political behaviour of simply 'ethical relativism' or 'ethical absolutism'. He castigates only a *certain type* of relativism and a *certain form* of absolutism as dangerous. Here he is quite right and it will be our purpose to clarify just what forms of these doctrines prove unfriendly to humane-libertarian political ideals.

Still, even some of Hofstadter's language proves disturb-ing to a political philosopher. He sums up his comments on Goldman by noting that: 'It is possible that the distinction between moral relativism and moral absolutism has been blurred because an excessively consistent practice of either leads to the same practical result—ruthlessness in political life.'[12] He seems to say that relativism needs to be countered with a measure of absolutism so that men will not bear evil quietly and that absolutism needs to be tempered by a measure of apathy and common sense or it may lead to fits of ruthless crusading.[13] Students, and even some lecturers, who read such passages often emerge with a strange notion of what ethical position they should adopt if they want to maximize their friendship for humane-libertarian ideals. Apparently, they should not fully espouse either ethical truth or ethical scepticism as the correct position or, if they feel forced to adopt one over the other in theory, they should at least refrain from being too consistent when it comes to practice. Ideally, they should be neither fish nor fowl but ready to sample both, that is, when they feel a fit of fanati-cism coming on they should take a bit of ethical relativism and when they find themselves unmoved by the latest case of police brutality they should try an absolute or two.

It is, of course, not Hofstadter's fault if people who are not clear about ethical distinctions get silly notions from reading a good book. Further, as he points out, it is not his business as a historian of reform to incorporate a treatise on the larger problems of political ethics.[14] This is perhaps unfortunate in that one can easily imagine sophisticated elaboration which would render Hofstadter's assertions both unobjectionable and useful. However, if it is not the historian's business to clarify ethical distinctions, it is our business and we *have* attempted to distinguish carefully what separates the doctrine of ethical truth from that of ethical scepticism. Let us see if our analysis can shed some light on how belief in one or the other is likely to affect a man's behaviour in regard to humane-libertarian ideals.

In Chapter 1, we learned that a man's position on the problem of ethical scepticism does not determine the *content* of his basic values; either a sceptic or a believer in ethical truth can hold either humane-libertarian ideals or Nietzschean ones. We also learned that his position does determine the *status* of his values: the believer in ethical truth feels that he can make a case that his basic values have objective or non-partisan status, that is, are worthy of regard from those who do not share them; while the sceptic denies that such a case can be made, holds that no one's values are worthy of regard except from those who appreciate them. And while granting that this difference in status is of little interest to certain men, we argued that others have a strong need to believe that their ideals have a higher status than those of their opponents. Now, if all of this is correct, it seems to follow that men who believe in ethical truth will tend to have a higher *esprit de corps* in regard to their ideals than sceptics, at least in statistical terms. Not that a sceptic's *esprit de corps* must be low. As we have seen, he need not be a nihilist; he can fight for his basic ideals with the full fervour that he derives from his emotional commitment to them. But a significant number of believers in ethical truth will enjoy *both* this sort of fervour (that which they derive from the strength of their commitments) *and* the gratification they derive from the belief that their ideals have more than partisan status! In sum, although we cannot speak with assurance of any particular individual, it appears that a population will enjoy a higher overall level of *esprit de corps* if they believe in ethical truth, other factors being equal, of course. Again, they will *add* to their emotional commitment to their ideals the *extra fervour* many of them derive from the conviction that their cause is a non-partisan one.

Our analysis leads, then, straight to this conclusion: believers in ethical truth tend to be both the best friends and the worst enemies of humane-libertarian values, depending on the *content* of their ideals. If they espouse an ideal inimical to humane-libertarian values, let us say a Nietzschean ideal, they will fight for *it* with the extra fervour of those who believe that their cause is a non-partisan one. But if they hold friendly ideals, e.g. Jeffersonian ones, they will fight for *those* with the same sort of heightened fervour. In other words, no blanket indictment of belief in ethical truth as subversive of humane conduct, or civil liberties, or tolerance, is valid. In fact, in times when humane-libertarian ideals have powerful enemies, their friends may well need to muster all the dedication they can in their defence—and thus, belief in ethical truth may prove a welcome ally. It will be a sad day if ever the humane become sceptics while the non-humane remain believers in ethical truth—if ever 'the best lack all conviction, while the worst are full of passionate intensity'.

No doubt, many readers will be disinclined to abandon the notion that belief in ethical truth tends to promote intolerance without further discussion. We can easily imagine a critic arguing as follows: 'Certainly, men who believe that their values are worthy of regard from those who do not share them are going to tend towards rigidity and intolerance in both social space and time. They will be inclined to ignore differences in situation, class, and culture. Thus, they will want to live by the code appropriate to their own environment when operating in other environments; indeed, they will want to judge other classes and nations in terms of their own code and even force it upon others. Such men will be equally inclined to resist the evolution of culture. They will fail to see the need, as mankind and the human condition alter, for changes that take us beyond all of our current values. Finally, as for the fact that believers in ethical truth tend to have a higher *esprit de corps* than sceptics, this is more dangerous than you admit. It may be that those humane men who possess the greatest fervour fight hardest on behalf of humane-libertarian values; but this is beneficial only if they are operating in a social context in which those values are appropriate. Often, their high *esprit de corps* encourages a crusading fanaticism that aims at forcing men to be free, that tries to force men to be humane and libertarian even though their cultural traditions provide no fertile soil for such ideals. Look at how often Jeffersonians in America have donned the shining armour of Wilsonian idealism, particularly when operating on the international scene; look at their imperialist crusades to make the world safe for democracy.'

In reply, as we have already seen, there is nothing about believing that one's ideals are in accord with ethical truth which *logically* entails projecting a narrowly defined code of behaviour into inappropriate situations; humane men can be flexible about calculating what specific actions will best serve their basic values in a particular situation *whether or not* they think they can justify those values against an opponent who does not share them. As to whether those who think that their basic values have non-partisan status will possess a *psychological* tendency to fail to adjust them to various situations, I am quite willing to concede that such men are likely to hold their ideals with unusual fervour. But from this, it does not obviously follow that they will tend to be rigid about their ideals; it seems to me just as likely that the more passionately a man feels about his basic values, the more ingenuity he will use to make them truly relevant to new situations. There are plenty of passionately humane men who do not delude themselves that a certain economic system or parliamentary democracy can be shuttled back and forth across cultural boundaries. They study each nation in turn in the hope of finding indigenous tendencies which may bring humane developments, perhaps well in the future. And they recognize that certain 'primitive' cultures may well be too rigid to alter significantly, even in a humane direction, without bringing on mass demoralization and that therefore, the most humane thing to do is to leave them alone.

The question of whether or not believers in ethical truth will resist the notion of cultural evolution, will be unwilling to see mankind transcend even their basic values, depends on the *kind* of ethical truth they believe in. I have already granted that those who follow non-empirical roads to ethical truth do tend to hold up certain 'truths' about values as final and certain. But again, Aristotelians (such as myself) *actually promote* the notion of human history as evolutionary, as an experiment which continually furnishes new data about ethical truth.* That is, while we hold (as probable) that a certain way of life has most perfected man thus far, we also endorse the proposition that mankind may go on to discover new ways of life which suit man better and better. And needless to say, our espousal of an empirical method of gaining ethical knowledge carries with it the whole ethos of free inquiry and tolerance that goes with belief in the scientific method. In fact, given the ambiguity and open-ended character of human history, there is every reason to tolerate societies which explore options we think unpromising. We can learn something from them, even if it is only that a certain way of life really is degrading ; and they may afford us some surprises.

Concerning the above critic's last point, that humane men who believe that their way of life is the most promising

---

* Again, the reader will have to wait until Chapter 5 for this notion to be elaborated.

(specifically Jeffersonians) tend to force their ideals upon others, if this were true, it would indeed be a serious indictment. For if there is anything that history does teach us, it is that those who think that they can use force or war to 'reform' others end up producing the most inhuman consequences (with rare exceptions) and thus betray their humane ideals. However, note that this lesson is incorporated into the *very core* of the Jeffersonian ideal; that is, while Jeffersonians certainly believe that some men are more perfect than others, they also hold that we are likely to maximize human perfection if we leave each individual free to lead his own life. Thus, a logical extension of Jeffersonianism to international politics would suggest that each society should be left to improve itself and that while a humane man may seek to influence other peoples as an ideologue or agitator or revolutionary, he will not call upon his nation-state as an instrument of coercion. Which in turn suggests that crusading Wilsonian idealism is a perversion of Jeffersonianism, a matter of men who hold very different values using the Jeffersonian ideal for their own purposes. After all, every nation includes ethnocentric and nationalistic types—and such men of course use the prevailing ideology to justify their imperialism. It is true that they used Jeffersonianism in the cases of America's entrance into World War I and U.S. intervention in Vietnam; but at the turn of the century when a savage, semi-Nietzschean Social Darwinism enjoyed a period of dominance, they were equally ready to utilize *that* to justify the Spanish–American War and the hey-day of gunboat diplomacy.

A final objection is frequently put: even if a sophisticated man who believes his ideals are in accord with ethical truth need not lean towards intolerance and ruthlessness, what of the fact that most believers are bound to be simplistic? Certainly these men are likely to think that they have a right to ram some sort of rigid code down the throats of others and thus, a rise in the number of believers will mean a rise in the level of ruthlessness. In answer, I ask what of the fact that most ethical relativists are likely to be equally simplistic?

These simplistic types, precisely because they *lack* a sophisticated grasp of what scepticism entails, precisely because they *do* think of it as reducing all ethical duties, obligations, and restraints to whims or tastes, are likely to react to it in terms of nihilism. Are nihilists such as Smerdyakov who think that 'anything is allowable' (that they have *carte blanche* to perpetrate any outrage) likely to be any less exploitive than those who think they have a right to bring salvation by the sword? And if the former are as bad as the latter, a shift of opinion in their favour is hardly going to improve things. At any rate, if the Jeffersonian ideal dominates the content of one's value system, and if one guards against the dangers of simplistic thinking, it is safe to be a thoroughly consistent believer in ethical truth. There is no reason to fear that one will suffer from too many fits of crusading fanaticism.

* * *

We must now deal with James's attempt to give the humane-libertarian ideal a new philosophical base, his attempt to found it on an acceptance, rather than a rejection, of the sceptic's position on ethical truth. As Ralph Barton Perry has pointed out, James wrote only one systematic essay on the problems of ethical theory, namely, 'The Moral Philosopher and the Moral Life'.[15] In this essay, significantly enough, James is almost completely preoccupied with the problems that ethical scepticism poses for his humane ideals.

James makes a good beginning by clearly distinguishing the question of the origins of our ethical ideas from the question of how we can deal with the ethical sceptic.[16] He thus avoids a trap. Recall why the reform Darwinists saw no alternative to value relativism. First, they believed that the views a man has about everything, including his views on good and evil, are nothing but a reflection of his socio-economic environment; that is, they accepted *sociological* relativism. Second, they assumed that any one who believed this had to become an ethical sceptic; that is, they equated sociological relativism with *philosophical* or 'truth' relativism. The second step, the equation, is the real trouble-maker. Note that it assumes that a causal hypothesis about the origins of our ethical ideas can decide the question of ethical truth versus scepticism.

This equation is a mistake. It may well be that the views that Aristotle and Newton had about astronomy were both a reflection of their respective environments, but this does not mean that preferring Newton over Aristotle is merely a matter of opinion. We feel that we can present an adequate defence of the scientific method (e.g. against the arguments of the 'Cartesian' sceptic) and therefore, the sociological relativism of the views of Newton and Aristotle does not disturb us. It merely means that Aristotle's environment prevented him from formulating hypotheses about astronomy as valid as those of Newton. Similarly, if we can present an adequate defence of a test for objectivity in ethics, we need not be disturbed by the sociological relativism of views about good and evil. It would merely mean, let us say, that Nietzsche's environment prevented him from developing ideals as worthy of regard as those of Aristotle. And if we *cannot* present an adequate defence of ethical truth, we do not need sociological relativism to turn us into ethical sceptics.

Unlike Veblen *et al.*, James had a real reason for feeling threatened by ethical scepticism; he believed that no one could present an adequate defence of ethical truth. However, he also believed that he could show that humane actions possess something more than partisan validity.

James gets his argument under way by telling us that what introduces value into the universe is the existence of sentient creatures who feel that certain things are good and make demands. He asserts that the very fact a man feels something to be good makes it good, good in the sense of good for him.[17] This phrase, 'good for him', is not one I would have chosen (see Chapter 1); however, James soon makes it clear that he uses it as I do 'valid only for him'.[18] In other words, the above assertion implies that *all* of the values or demands men actually internalize are good, but (at this point in the argument at least) good only in a *non-objective* sense. *Every* value is good in the sense of being worthy of regard from those who hold it but *not* from those who do not hold it. It seems to me that all James has said thus far is fair enough, *if* it is impossible to make a case for ethical truth, a case which would divide the differing values various men hold into those with objective status and those with only subjective status. And the impossibility of doing this is something James is about to try to demonstrate.

As for James's reasons for rejecting the possibility of a case for ethical truth, he scrutinizes a variety of such cases and finds them all lacking. First, there are those who believe that some sort of moral order resides in the 'nature of things', an order that can furnish us with a criterion which both possesses objective status and allows us to rank various human values as better or worse. James accuses these thinkers of an error which, although he does not use the term, amounts to committing the naturalistic fallacy, that is, arguing from facts to values.[19] Having disposed of such thinkers, he next lists a whole range of criteria, all of which rank human ideals or demands into hierarchy of value and all of which have been proposed as candidates for objective status. His list includes the tests of intuition, promoting the greatest happiness of the greatest number, preserving the human species, being in accord with a universal law, being in accord with the will of God, etc. James rejects them all as either inadequate or too vague.[20]

Having conceded that no one can present an adequate defence of objectivity in the realm of ethics, how is the philosopher to escape the world of the ethical sceptic? James poses this question and then immediately gives us his answer :[21]

> But do we not already see a perfectly definite path of escape which is open to him just because he is a philosopher, and not the champion of one particular ideal? Since everything which is demanded is by that fact a good, must not the guiding principle for ethical philosophy (since all demands conjointly cannot be satisfied in this poor

world) be simply to satisfy at all times *as many demands as we can*? That act must be the best act, accordingly, which makes for the *best whole*, in the sense of awakening the least sum of dissatisfactions.

So now, James has escaped the sceptic and justified his cherished humanism : we act best when we act humanely, that is, when we satisfy as many of the demands of men as we can and frustrate as few as we can.

James's way of stating his solution to the problem of scepticism engenders a problem of interpretation, one posed by the phrase '... just because he is a philosopher'. This phrase (and certain other passages), if taken at face-value, would mean that James is saying only that it is unfitting for members of the philosophical fraternity to champion certain ideals over others and that therefore, they should attempt to satisfy all human demands impartially. But is he really only formulating a code for philosophers about how to treat ideals, much as a doctor might recommend to his fellow physicians a code about how to treat patients, e.g. not to play favourites but to give impartial treatment to all as best they can? I find it hard to believe that James was only suggesting a professional code of ethics for philosophers. If so, we would hardly feel that his essay was a real attempt to deal with ethical scepticism. Certainly, he must want to justify his humane ideals for all men, not just philosophers. And soon enough, our surmise is proved correct. For James goes on to call his maxim that we should attempt to satisfy as many human demands as we can an 'unconditional commandment',[22] which implies that this maxim is worthy of regard from *all men* whatever their situation. Indeed, the rest of the passage tells us that not just the philosopher, but the non-philosopher, the statesman, the novelist, the minister, the reformer, etc., must *all* cast their vote for the richer (more satisfying) universe.[23]

It seems to me, then, that what is supposed to lead a man to endorse James's argument is not that he is a professional philosopher, but rather that he is 'philosopher' enough to

6

follow and appreciate the drift of James's philosophical analysis. And this analysis focuses upon establishing that all human values or demands are good and that no one can make a defensible case for ethical truth. In other words, I believe that the core of James's argument is this: (1) The fact a man actually holds a value or makes a demand renders it good, which is to say all human values or demands are good; (2) we cannot show that some value criteria are good in an objective sense while others are not; (3) which leaves us with our original assertion that *all* human values or demands are good—and this means that we should attempt to satisfy as many values as we can without discriminating against certain ones in terms of what they are or whose they are.

This argument appears plausible. If no one can show that we should discriminate in favour of certain values as objective and against others as subjective, must we not treat them all on a par? If no one can show that some demands are worthy of our regard while others are not, must we not (if all demands are good) treat them all as worthy of our regard? Further, James's argument confounds the sceptic so neatly. It grants the sceptic the concession he asks, that no man can present an adequate defence of ethical truth, and then uses that very concession to defeat him. The *very fact* no one can justify classifying values as objective or merely subjective is used to provide a justification of humane actions, actions which attempt to satisfy as many human demands as possible. Finally, the logic of the argument seems to be quite sound. The premiss asserts the *presumption* that all demands are good; the second step states the lack of validity of all positions contrary to that presumption, namely, all attempts to show that *only some* values are objectively good; and therefore, the conclusion reiterates the premiss, asserts *as confirmed* that all demands are good.

But does the conclusion reiterate the premiss? Actually, a subtle shift has taken place concerning *the sense* in which all demands are said to be good. Recall that when James introduced his premiss, it asserted that all the demands men made were good only in a *non-objective sense*. That is, every particular value, while good by virtue of the fact someone held it, was only 'good for him'—was worthy of regard *only by the man who held it*. If James had claimed anything more, we would not have conceded his point. For the fact a man holds a particular value does not make it worthy of regard from someone else who does not share it. James's conclusion, on the other hand, asserts that all demands are good in an *objective sense*. This is clear enough if we focus on how we are told we should act in regard to the demands of men. We are not being told that each of us has the right to regard our own internalized values as good and need respect the values of others only in so far as we share them (or espouse a humane code that includes respect for others). Rather, we are being told that we must respect the values or demands of others *without reference to whether their values are also ours*; and certainly, this is equivalent to saying that all demands are good in an objective sense. It is interesting to note that James begins to alter the sense in which all demands are said to be good precisely when he takes the second step in his argument, when he attempts to show that a defensible case for ethical truth is impossible. At that point, he says, 'the demand may be for anything under the sun'[24] (it makes no difference what the demand is for) and 'we must throw our own spontaneous ideals, even the dearest, impartially in with that total mass of ideals which are fairly to be judged'[25] (it makes no difference whether we hold the value or not).

If the above contention is correct, if there is a gap between James's premiss and his conclusion, the second step in his argument emerges as crucial. Can it bridge the gap between premiss and conclusion? I think not. James's second step simply asserts his acceptance of the sceptic's position on ethical truth, that is, it asserts that we cannot show that certain value criteria have objective status while others do not. One can hardly argue that our failure to show that *some* values have objective status justifies saying that *all* human values have objective status! Yet, once the gap between premiss and conclusion is made explicit, this is what James's argument amounts to. James criticizes previous thinkers for holding that certain values were objective, but he packs more objective status into the realm of ethics than any of his predecessors. Again, his argument amounts to saying that accepting ethical scepticism entails attributing objective status to *all* human demands. This is certainly peculiar, given that scepticism is a doctrine which holds that *no* values possess objectivity.

James himself assumes that his second step, his acceptance of the sceptic's position on ethical truth, takes him back to his premiss. And so it should. For his premiss says that all human demands have only non-objective status, which is precisely the position of the sceptic. What else would accepting ethical scepticism entail except ethical scepticism? James's argument leaves him where he begins, caught in the universe of the sceptic, a universe in which each man's basic values have only partisan validity and in which no one need respect the values of others unless he shares them.

Of course, there is an alternative to asserting that men should attempt to maximize the satisfactions of mankind on the grounds that all human demands possess objective status. One can simply assert this as an overriding ethical principle, that is, one can *simply state* 'men should attempt to fulfil as many human demands as possible', just as one might state 'men should not steal' as a substantive ethical principle. At times, James seems to do this. Remember that he refers to satisfying human demands as an unconditional *commandment*. And this raises the question : have we missed something in James's argument? If James thinks of his 'unconditional commandment' as merely an ethical principle with a certain distinctive content (a content that calls for treating all demands of all men as equally worthy of satisfaction), perhaps the *sort of content* of the criteria he rejects is central to his argument. Indeed, if we look back to his account of the criteria he rejects, we find a heavy emphasis on the fact that these criteria favour certain values over others, that they order values into a hierarchy. This line of reasoning suggests a simple two-step argument on James's behalf: (1) No one can justify a value criterion which puts certain demands ahead of others (e.g. artistic values ahead of feeding the hungry) or the demands of certain men ahead of the demands of others (e.g. those of supermen ahead of those of herd men—examples mine); (2) this lends justification to a criterion which treats all human demands as worthy of satisfaction without reference to what they are or whose they are.

From experience, I know that many find this new argument convincing: They say: 'After all, if men have no reason to rank demand A above demand B, should they not treat them as equal in value?' But James has done nothing to show that men have *no reason* to rank demands; those men who hold élitist criteria have reason to do so—because of the criteria they hold. All James has attempted to show is that the élitist can present *no justification* of his criterion, no case that it possesses objective status. And this leaves the élitist with no reason *only if* he must discount his criterion in the absence of such a case. However, he need not, assuming of course that no one, élitist or equalitarian, can make a case for ethical truth. Again, scepticism does not entail nihilism. Thus, if the sceptic is correct, the élitist can turn to his criterion for reasons precisely as valid as those equalitarians derive from their criteria. Both can give partisan reasons for whether or not they rank human demands.

James might reply that we have missed the point of his argument, namely, that the fact the élitist cannot justify his value criterion *lends justification* to an equalitarian criterion. But does it? How does the fact that the élitist cannot defend his criterion against the sceptic afford us a defence of an equalitarian criterion? The fact that non-humane men cannot make a case for the objective status of *their* criteria hardly provides those of us who are humane with a case for the objective status of *our* criterion. If presented with this version of James's argument, any sceptic worth his salt would ask: 'All right, the élitists have failed to make a case against me, now where is your case? Certainly, you don't mean to say that their failure saves you the trouble of presenting a case on your own behalf?' I can see no answer to the sceptic's question in James's essay. This of course does not mean that James must give up his humane commandment. But his failure to make a case for ethical truth does mean that he must grant that his criterion has only non-objective status—and that he is still caught in the world of the sceptic. It means that when faced with a non-humane opponent, a Nietzschean let us say, he can claim no advantage in terms of justification.

In sum, when faced with a non-humane opponent, there are two ways in which James can justify his assertion that all human demands are worthy of respect: either by showing that a *principle* which asserts this possesses objective status, or by showing that all human demands *themselves* have objective status. Instead, James concedes that no defensible case for objectivity in ethics is possible and proposes two fallacious arguments, fallacious precisely because they leap the gap between non-objective and objective status without any real justification. Or better, *I suspect* that both of these arguments run through James's essay. For I must concede that he does not consciously distinguish them; the second seems not so much a separate entity as interwoven with the first, that is, its steps seem to be used merely to reinforce the reasoning of the first. Perhaps it would be best to attribute to James only the first argument criticized above and therefore, level at him only one line of criticism: that what he does is equivalent to saying that scepticism entails treating all human demands as if they had objective status.

*　　*　　*

Our analysis of James's argument reveals something of considerable theoretical interest: his mistake is the *mirror-image* of one we diagnosed earlier, namely, the mistake of those who argue that ethical scepticism logically entails nihilism. Just as they assumed that scepticism means treating all values as if they had *failed* a test of objectivity, James effectively assumes that scepticism means treating all values as if they had *passed* a test of objectivity!

James's argument is as persistent as it is fallacious. American social scientists right up to the present day formulate vulgarized versions of it (quite independently of any knowledge of James). Time after time, we open their books to read something like this: 'Ethical relativism means that our values are no more objective than anyone else's; therefore, we should respect the values of others as much as our own. In a word, we should be tolerant. And since tolerance is the soul of humane behaviour and political freedom, humanism must be founded on the doctrine of ethical relativism.' These arguments are of such immense contemporary influence that they deserve a special name: perhaps, the 'tolerance school fallacy'. And we have learned to pin-point the fallacy: scepticism does *not* entail respecting the values of others regardless of whether one shares them; scepticism does *not* allow one to accord tolerance objective status any more than intolerance. One just cannot conjure up the objectivity that belongs to ethical truth by a rejection of ethical truth. In so far as these arguments hold that scepticism *logically entails* tolerance of the values of others, they are patently absurd.

Certain men may well have a *psychological reaction* to scepticism along the above lines, although since such a reaction is not logically entailed it is primarily an indication that they already had a proclivity towards tolerance. An equally possible psychological reaction is the following: 'Scepticism means that no one else's values are worthy of my regard; therefore, I have a right to be as exploitive as I please.' It is vital to distinguish understandable psychological reactions to scepticism from what it logically entails. Confusing these two things provides the tolerance school fallacy with its power to persuade, for a tolerant psychological reaction to scepticism is quite understandable—at least from a certain personality type. And the same sort of confusion deceives those who argue that scepticism entails nihilism. For nihilism is a frequent psychological reaction to scepticism. As we have seen, this is certainly true of the unsophisticated who leap to the conclusion that 'anything is allowable'; but it can be true of others as well. While sophisticated men usually react only by way of diminished *esprit de corps*, they can react in terms of a dark and savage disillusion—*if* their morale is *totally* bound up with the notion that their ideals have objective status. Indeed, it is quite possible that reactions to scepticism do more for exploitation and nihilism than for tolerance and humanism. I want to underscore this. I have been so eager to show that belief in ethical truth need not have obnoxious psychological effects that I have neglected to emphasize the bad effects scepticism can have.

Despite its flaws, the persistence of James's argument is easily explained. Humane men, both in America and elsewhere, keep inventing it (or better, their own variations on it) because it seems to offer an escape from the hard realities of scepticism. It fosters the illusion that one can accept ethical scepticism and still justify one's humane values. Those Jeffersonians who need to feel that their ideals have objective status would do well to abandon illusions and face up to their hard task: they will have to build a foundation for their political ideal out of a case for ethical truth. No conjurer's trick can keep their ideal aloft for long, even when the conjurer is as skilled and polished as William James.

NOTES

[1] See Robert Allen Rutland, *The Birth of the Bill of Rights, 1776–1791* (Chapel Hill: The University of North Carolina Press, 1955), Chapter IV.

[2] Quoted in Richard Hofstadter, *The American Political Tradition* (New York: Alfred A. Knopf, 1957), p. 43.

[3] Eric F. Goldman, *Rendezvous with Destiny* (Revised ed.; New York: Vintage Books, 1956), pp. 66–72. The author has drawn heavily upon Goldman in his attempt to isolate the drift of American social thought in the late nineteenth century concerning ethical truth. This attempt to extract a single line of thought from its setting has introduced a distortion which is, of course, not present in Goldman's full and balanced account.

[4] *Ibid.*, pp. 72–6. The reference to Westermarck may cause surprise.

However, while most of Westermarck's work belongs to the twentieth century, the book that so pleased the conservative Social Darwinists was his first, *The History of Human Marriage* (1891).

5 Thorstein Veblen, *The Theory of the Leisure Class* (New York: Macmillan, 1899), pp. 34, 97–8. For an excellent discussion of Veblen's position on value judgments, see Morton G. White, *Social Thought in America* (New York: The Viking Press, 1952), Chapter VI.

6 Goldman, *op. cit.*, p. 156.

7 Walter Lippmann, *A Preface to Politics* (New York and London: M. Kennerley, 1913).

8 Indeed, Lippmann eventually came to believe that his political ideals *must* rest on a foundation of ethical truth. See particularly Walter Lippmann, *The Public Philosophy* (Boston: Little, Brown, and Co., 1955).

9 Goldman, *op. cit.*, pp. 215–17.

10 James's address to the Yale Philosophical Club, 'The Moral Philosopher and the Moral Life', was first published in the *International Journal of Ethics*, April 1891.

11 Richard Hofstadter, *The Age of Reform* (New York: Alfred A. Knopf, 1956), p. 15.

12 *Ibid.*, p. 16.

13 *Ibid.*, pp. 15–16.

14 *Ibid.*, p. 322n.

15 William James, *Essays on Faith and Morals*, ed. Ralph Barton Perry (New York: Longmans, Green, and Co., 1943), p. v.

16 James, *The Will to Believe*, pp. 184–6.

17 *Ibid.*, pp. 190–1.   18 *Ibid.*, pp. 191–2.

19 *Ibid.*, pp. 193, 196–7.   20 *Ibid.*, pp. 199–201.

21 *Ibid.*, p. 205.   22 *Ibid.*, p. 209.

23 *Ibid.*, p. 210.   24 *Ibid.*, p. 201.

25 *Ibid.*, p. 199.

4

Hobbes and Modern Natural Right

If today's Jeffersonians cannot depend on James for a case in favour of the objective validity of their humane-libertarian ideal, what of Locke and Rousseau, the founders of the doctrine of modern natural right? After all, this doctrine provided the original ethical foundation on which the Jeffersonian ideal was constructed and further, it continues to possess a powerful appeal. If we look at the Universal Declaration of Human Rights, adopted by the U.N. General Assembly in 1948, we find both an expression of the humane-libertarian ideal and a justification of that ideal —and the latter is stated in language strongly reminiscent of Locke and Rousseau.[1] Staughton Lynd, the historian and agitator, has detailed the extent to which the New Left in America calls upon the doctrine of natural right, albeit a radicalized version of it. Perhaps the Jeffersonians of yesterday were too hasty in abandoning the foundation of their political ideal? Lynd argues as much.[2]

I share with many other political philosophers the conviction that the doctrine of modern natural right is not philosophically defensible, the conviction that certain critics, particularly John Stuart Mill and R. H. Tawney, have shown this doctrine to be radically defective. I intend to rehearse and supplement the arguments of these critics to indicate why they have been found convincing. However, I want to do more than criticize modern natural right. For

80

it is sometimes assumed that the critique which disposes of that doctrine is equally effective against the doctrine of classical natural law. As a step towards defending the viability of natural law, this chapter will attempt to show that Locke and Rousseau are vulnerable, *not* in so far as their approach resembles that of Plato and Aristotle, but because their approach was dictated by *Hobbes* and that therefore, the vulnerability of their doctrine does not necessarily carry over to natural law. Indeed, it will be argued that the legacy of Hobbes is so potent that Plato and Aristotle actually could have *endorsed* the critique usually levelled against Locke and Rousseau.

*   *   *

How did Hobbes set the stage for the rise of modern natural right? He did this primarily by formulating a powerful critique of classical natural law or, more exactly, he formulated a powerful critique of the doctrine of essences. For natural law, as developed by Plato and Aristotle and their medieval disciples, was founded upon the doctrine of essences. The best way of elucidating this point is to take a look at the early Plato. *The Republic* approaches the problem of what way of life is best for man by attempting to discover the nature of justice. This makes sense in that justice is conceived of as the ordering principle of human society, the principle according to which each man is assigned his social role, benefits, and responsibilities ; thus, it provides the key to a society's way of life. Plato rejects Thrasymachus' method of discovering the nature of justice, namely, generalizing on the basis of a study of actual human societies. Since all actual human societies are ordered to some degree by the struggle for power, such a method leads to a concept of justice as 'might makes right'. Rather Plato holds that one must transcend actual human societies, which are a mixture of perfection and imperfection, to study the general Idea of human society within whose content one can find the perfect state of human society, that is, human society ordered in terms of justice. It is, then, within the content of the general Ideas that we find the perfect state of things, what a thing *really is*, in a word, its nature or *essence*.

An analogy drawn from mathematics may prove helpful. All straight lines in the physical world have minute crooks and bends in them, that is, no actual straight line is really perfectly straight. In so far as they lack perfection, they fall short of what a straight line really is, namely, the shortest distance between two points. If we want to find the *essence* of a straight line, we must turn to the geometer's Idea of a straight line, for only there will we find a line that is more than a mixture of what a straight line is and is not. Similarly, all actual human societies are a mixture of perfection and imperfection, of what society really is and what it is not. In so far as an actual human society is ordered by the struggle for power, it is an anti-social collection of men, falls short of the essence of human society. In so far as an actual human society is ordered by justice, allots social roles in accord with merit and rights in accord with social roles, it is a true community of men, realizes the essence of human society. But again, if we want to discover human society in its perfect state, we must look to the philosopher's general Idea of human society, for only there will we find the *essence* of human society unblemished by existence in the physical world.

Plato, at least the early Plato, believed that general Ideas or essences had more than conceptual existence, that they corresponded to an objectively existing world of Forms. Aristotle demurred from this, that is, he held that general Ideas or essences had only conceptual existence except in so far as they were imperfectly realized by actual things existing in the physical world. However, as this statement implies, Aristotle followed Plato in founding ethics on the concept of man's nature or essence. If a society's way of life is to be accorded more than conventional value, it must do a better job than other ways of life in helping men to realize the potentialities of their nature. Aristotle also endorsed a second basic contention of Plato's ethics, namely, that men must develop 'spirit' or moral indignation or a sense of honour if they are to resist the temptations of passion or desire, temptations that lead men away from the perfecting life. Only if men are taught to *feel* moral approval of right actions and moral revulsion at wrong actions can they resist the powerful emotive force of desire.

In sum, for Plato and Aristotle the solution to the problem posed by the fact that human beings and societies differ about fundamental values or what way of life is best was this : that one can draw a distinction between the *natural* (what is *objectively* best for man whether he realizes it or not) and the *conventional* (whatever men happen to value). And they drew this distinction in terms of the doctrine of essences, that is, the natural was what best realized the potentialities of man's nature or essence, what (for Aristotle) maximized man's felicity or sense of fulfilment. Or better, they drew this distinction within the context of a four-fold phenomenal world, which included: (1) General Ideas or essences ; (2) the physical world, the actual world of sense and sense images ; (3) spirit or moral indignation, feelings of 'should be' and 'should not be' ; (4) the passions or desires. For future reference, it is worth emphasizing that their distinction between the natural and the conventional *was not* drawn in terms of pre-social man versus socialized man, but rather in terms of socially perfected man versus socially debased man. Both Plato and Aristotle assumed that one could discover the perfection of man only by viewing him in the context of a perfect or just human society. And further, keep in mind their contention that the distinction between the natural and the conventional *could not* be drawn within the context of the actual world ; even at its best the actual world of men falls short of full realization of man's essence.

Hobbes was thoroughly aware that classical natural law was founded on the doctrine of essences and that therefore, a refutation of the latter would do much to discredit the former. His attack on the doctrine of essences consists of three arguments, which are drawn together in Part III of the *Leviathan* in a chapter delightfully entitled, 'Of Darkness from Vain Philosophy and Fabulous Traditions'. These three arguments may be classified in terms of their line of attack as linguistic, metaphysical, and epistemological.

The linguistic argument has to do with the meaning of what Hobbes calls common names or universals, like 'chair', as distinct from singular names, like 'that chair'. Sometimes we use the word 'chair' to refer to a whole class of objects rather than a particular object, as when we say 'chairs are less expensive than beds'. Plato held that the meaning of such common names could only be explained by way of the doctrine of general Ideas or essences. He argued that when a word like 'chair' is used to refer to a whole class of differing particular chairs, it must stand for an Idea whose content is *general enough* to *allow for* all the differences between particular chairs. For example, the general Idea of chair would have to leave undefined such characteristics of chairs as their exact height, weight, colour, etc. For certainly a thing does not have to be three feet high, or weigh ten pounds, or be blue in order to be a chair. This means that the general Idea of chair cannot be reduced to a sense-image in that a sense-image does define size, colour, etc., that is, it is a sense-image of a blue or a brown or a green chair and thus, it would exclude certain chairs from the class chair. For Plato, then, the Idea of chair must be truly general, for example, we might say that a chair is a material object that elevates a surface suited to the seated human form to a convenient height.

Hobbes offers us a very different analysis of the meaning of such common names. He tells us that there is 'nothing in the world universal but names' and further that: 'One universal name is imposed on many things for their similitude in some quality or other accident; and whereas a proper name brings to mind one thing only, universals recall any one of those many.'[3] In other words, we put differing particular chairs in the class chair, not because they fall under one general Idea, but because they share a resemblance to one another. And when we say 'chairs are less expensive than beds', the common name 'chairs' does not call to mind some general Idea but merely a representative sense-image of a particular chair, a sense-image that represents the class chair rather as a poll-taker's sample represents a whole population. Hobbes concludes that the names of things are always the names of sense impressions or remembered sense-images, which is to say he espouses nominalism and denies any need to posit general Ideas or essences as an explanation of the meaning of language.[4]

Hobbes also denies that essences play any metaphysical role, that is, he rejects the contention that they exist or that they are needed to explain what differentiates existing things. Hobbes was much impressed by the work of Galileo and the pioneers of modern science. He was convinced that the model of the world that they found useful in their scientific pursuits, the world as composed of bodies in motion, held the clue as to what the world was really like. Indeed, he seems to have held some sort of crude atomic theory. A chair appears to us to be a continuous brown expanse, but it is really composed of material particles and our sense impressions of it are mere appearances. Our emotions, like our sensations, are not bodies and therefore, they too are not real but are merely an epiphenomenon that arises out of the interaction of bodies in motion. Perhaps this is why Hobbes lumps all human emotions together as mere fancy or desire, that is, fails to draw any qualitative distinction between man's moral feelings, his feelings of spirit or moral indignation, and his desires.

At any rate, Hobbes's metaphysics was antagonistic to the doctrine of essences. The ancients themselves asserted that the essence of a thing could not be found in the physical universe and was not to be identified with a concrete parti-cular thing. For Hobbes, such an assertion, an assertion that essences were not bodies, was equivalent to an admission that essences did not exist.[5] Finally, one did not need essences to explain how things differed from one another, that is, one did not need to follow the ancients and say that a man differed from a stone because the former partook of the nature of man while the latter partook of the essence of stone. For Hobbes, the difference between a man and a stone could be explained in terms of their atomic structure. Perhaps a man's component bodies were arranged in a circular pattern and moved clockwise, while a stone's bodies were arranged in a square and moved counter-clockwise.

While Hobbes does not explicitly use his epistemology to refute the doctrine of essences, it is equally antagonistic to that doctrine. Since he believes that only body in motion is real, he concludes, not unnaturally, that science and mathematics are the only roads to knowledge of reality. This leaves no room for knowledge of essences in that, as Plato argued against Thrasymachus, one cannot discover the essence or nature of things by way of scientific generalization, but must proceed to a dialectical analysis of the general Ideas. Further, as Hobbes points out, science proper is limited to *describing* things and establishing their causes and effects.[6] This also holds for the values of men, that is, science can describe them but cannot evaluate them, cannot say that one man's values are closer to the truth about good and evil than another's. Hobbes feels, then, that he has sufficient grounds to dismiss the ethics of Plato and Aristotle as a mere rationalization of their likes and dislikes.[7] First, science allows for no evaluative knowledge of values; and second, with the fall of the doctrine of essences, Plato and Aristotle can no longer evaluate the values and conventions of men in terms of which values serve to perfect man's nature or essence. The illegitimacy of elevating certain values over others, except in terms of one's own preferences, extends of course to moral values, which may be another reason why Hobbes does not distinguish spirit or moral value from other sorts of value, for example, man's desires.[8]

Before we leave Hobbes, we must take stock of the overall effects of his critique of the doctrine of essences. What Hobbes had done was nothing less than this: he had collapsed the four-fold phenomenal world of the ancients, a world of essences, sensation, spirit, and desire, into a two-fold world of sense and desire. In doing this, he had destroyed the foundations of classical political ethics in that the classical distinction between the natural (what is objectively best in terms of perfecting man's nature) and the conventional (whatever men happen to value) could not be drawn in terms of sense and desire.

It might seem, in view of my espousal of neo-Aristotelianism, that I ought to offer a detailed answer to Hobbes's critique of the ancients. Actually, I feel that I can be very brief. Most contemporary philosophers would attack Hobbes on the following grounds: that nominalism does not remove the need to posit true universals; that scientifically useful concepts should not be converted into a metaphysics; and that the mathematical sciences do not exhaust human knowledge. They would, of course, hasten to add that Hobbes was correct in rejecting the doctrine of essences as a metaphysics. However, as the reader will recall, I too reject classical metaphysics. I am interested in reviving natural law concepts, such as that of the essence or nature of man, neither as concepts that correspond to a transcendent world of Forms nor as something whose 'contents' hold the key to knowledge of good and evil. I want to use them as concepts which can afford us a rewarding ethical interpretation of the story of mankind, concepts which can help us to learn from mankind's experience with thousands of ways of life. There are strong objections to my approach, and no doubt some of them are foreshadowed in a rough way in Hobbes's critique, but I would prefer to wait until the next two chapters and deal with them in their most modern and sophisticated form.

As for our understanding of the plight of Locke and Rousseau, what is of significance is not whether Hobbes was right but that he carried the day. The founders of modern natural right took a fatal step: they followed Hobbes into his world of sense and desire and rejected the four-fold phenomenal world of the ancients.

However, these same thinkers were not willing to follow Hobbes towards the sceptical conclusions that he drew from his critique of the ancients. The extent of Hobbes's scepticism is a matter of debate among scholars, but there is no

7

doubt that his rejection of the classical distinction between the natural and the conventional led him at times to speak of ethics as if it were merely conventional, as if good and evil were *defined* by the civil law of the state.[9] This leaves the individual without much of a criterion to judge or condemn the actions of his sovereign; indeed, Hobbes tells us that there is no objective distinction between a king and a tyrant[10] and further, that there is no difference between the rights of a constituted sovereign and one who has achieved power by conquest.[11] While a sophisticated interpretation of Hobbes requires discussion or qualification of such passages, this much is clear: Hobbes reduced the rights of the individual to one, the right to resist the sovereign if he threatens your life.[12] And even this 'right' seems to be more a matter of enlightened self-interest than principle in that a criminal, however justly condemned, is correct to use force to save himself.[13] Presumably, even a murderer has a 'right' to take innocent life in order to resist arrest.

*　　*　　*

Thus, after Hobbes, the stage was set for a new attempt to draw the distinction between the natural and the conventional, a step that might restore the foundations of ethics and political freedom, that might justify humane behaviour and the rights of the individual versus the state. But this new attempt would have to take place *within Hobbes's universe* of sense and desire and therefore, would have to result in something very different from the classical distinction between the natural and the conventional. And indeed, Locke and Rousseau *do* present us with a very different sort of distinction, that is, they identify the natural with *pre-social* man and the conventional with *socialized* man. Their thinking runs along these lines: Socialized man is man's man, a product of what man has made of himself. For society is a human creation and thus, man as a social product is a creation of man's own perhaps arbitrary values and conventions. But, if we can only perform a certain conceptual experiment, if we can only look at man and strip away what society has done to him, the pre-social residue will be God's man, man as he came from the hand of God. This natural man can be identified with goodness, for God does nothing save what is good, and therefore, natural man will furnish us with a criterion of good and evil that we can use to evaluate the conventions of society and the laws of the state.

While Locke and Rousseau share the same general approach to the problem of how to derive a criterion of good and evil that will have more than conventional status, they differ on many points. The most fundamental difference, in my opinion, has to do with *which part* of Hobbes's universe of sense and desire they explore in their search for a criterion. Locke turns primarily to the *realm of sense*, that is, the world of physical nature including man as part of that world. He hopes to subtract from the physical world everything that man has done to it, to imagine it minus knives and forks and ploughed fields and human societies, and, once he envisions God's unmarred creation, to find an indication therein of the purposes of God. It is rather as if we stripped a Frank Lloyd Wright building of all the additions later added on, so that we could divine the inspiration of the original design. Rousseau, on the other hand, turns to Hobbes's *realm of desire* for his distinction between the natural and the conventional, that is, he tries to distinguish man's natural desires, man's *instincts*, from man's conventional desires, the values *society* has engendered in man. This means that Rousseau focuses mostly on man, rather than on physical nature inclusive of man as did Locke. Further, when Rousseau envisions God's man, pre-social or instinctive man, he does not speculate much about God's purposes. He takes it for granted that if God gave man certain instincts, God meant man to follow them.

Let us first take a look at Locke. In his early unpublished essays on the law of nature, Locke tells us why he did not embark on the path similar to that later taken by Rousseau, that is, why he rejects the notion that man has instinctive knowledge of virtue. He holds that if the law of nature were written on the hearts of men, one would expect primitive peoples, who have not been corrupted by civilized conventions, to be exemplars of good conduct; in fact, however, they are a thoroughly brutal and impious lot.[14] Thus, Locke feels obliged to turn elsewhere to find the law of nature and argues 'that the foundation of all knowledge of it is derived from those things which we perceive through our senses'.[15] When we do focus on God's creation, we will not find ourselves at a loss to discover his intentions for 'he has not created this world for nothing and without purpose'.[16] The approach of these early essays is reflected in all of Locke's later major works;[17] for example, in the *First Treatise on Civil Government*, he censures those whose principles cannot 'be made to agree with that constitution and order which God had settled in the world'.[18] It is worth noting, however, that Locke does not always confine his attention to the realm of sense. Both his early and his later works occasionally cite certain human instincts as evidence of God's intentions much in the manner of Rousseau, a fact that gives point to some of Rousseau's criticisms of Locke.[19]

What then, according to Locke, are the world and man like when they come from the hand of God and what rights and duties did God intend man to acknowledge? As for duties, the very majesty of God's creations display his power and wisdom and he intends us to honour him. He created all men with an instinct for self-preservation and thus implied a duty to preserve our own lives and to respect the lives of others.[20] This latter duty is reinforced by the very fact that all men are God's creations and that he certainly did not make things merely to be destroyed. The fact that certain creatures, plants and animals, have been created inferior to man shows that God intended them for man's use but again, they are not meant to be destroyed or wasted.[21] As for human rights, God created all men free and equal, that is, he created them all of the same species and gave no man a sceptre as a sign that he was to rule over others. Thus, men have a right to be ruled only by their own consent.[22] Since no man has the power of life and death even over himself, no one has such a power over anyone else, which is to say men have a right to be free from enslavement.[23] That God intended men to be free is further evidenced by the fact that he gave them free will. Finally, God did not create the earth divided into sections and deeded to specific individuals, indeed, he created man with only one possession, his body and the labour of that body. Therefore, men have a right to the property with which they mix their labour, except under conditions of scarcity.[24]

At this point, readers familiar with Locke may wish to pose an objection. Unlike Hobbes, Locke argues that men living in a state of nature, men who have not yet contracted a government, could form co-operative human societies. How then, you might ask, can I argue that Locke envisions man in a pre-social state when he attempts to derive his ethics? In answer, Locke does *not* derive his ethics from his state of nature, which is indeed a social state; rather, the *social character* of his state of nature is *based on* his ethics, and his ethics *is derived* from envisioning man in a pre-social state. What Locke does is this: *After* deriving his ethics by envisioning man and nature as they come from the hand of God, he performs a *second* conceptual experiment. He imagines men living without civil government but with the ability to learn about their natural right and duties. In so far as such men know and live by that code, they can avoid war and anarchy and enjoy the blessings of human society. This gives Locke a powerful argument against Hobbes, who told men that they had to choose between civil government and a state of nature which was pure anarchy and that therefore, they had best not overthrow the sovereign unless their very lives were threatened. Locke argues that the state of nature is not all that bad and that therefore, men ought to demand a lot more than self-preservation in return for tolerating the sovereign's rule.

In sum, we find in Locke: (1) Man and nature as they

came from the hand of God, from whence Locke derives his ethics; (2) man in the state of nature living socially thanks to a shared ethics; and (3) man in civil society, where government serves, if it does its job, to remove some of the causes of social instability which plague the state of nature. It is perhaps necessary to make explicit that Locke does *not* think that man as he comes from the hand of God ever actually existed in history; for Locke, he is purely a *conceptual experiment*. He does not represent a state of human development, what man was like at some actual moment (e.g. the Garden of Eden) when he came from the hand of God; rather, he is a device to help Locke draw the line between the natural and the conventional. As for man living socially in the state of nature, Locke sometimes treats him as historical, but seems half-hearted about it. I do not at present want to commit myself as to whether Locke means us to take him as purely a conceptual experiment or as historical fact as well. There is no doubt that Locke uses him primarily to justify limits on the power of the state; whether he is more effective for that purpose when thought of as an actual or merely conceptual alternative to civil society is a difficult question. Finally, man in civil society is, of course, not a conceptual experiment but is typical of the condition in which men actually live.

Rousseau's attempt to find an ethics in Hobbes's realm of desire gets off to an unpromising start. In his earliest important work, the first Discourse (*Discourse on the Arts and Sciences*), he baldly identifies good with savage man and evil with civilized man: savages are said to possess simplicity, temperance, fidelity, and courage, while civilized man is characterized by conformity, hypocrisy, suspicion, jealousy, deceit, and, worst of all, philosophical scepticism.[25] It did not take Rousseau long to retreat from this position, and for good reason. As Locke had pointed out, it is not difficult to find some extremely unpleasant savages. Further, if civilized society is purely evil in its influence, the only solution for man is to revert to savagery, an unpalatable alternative.

In his second Discourse (*Discourse on the Origin of Inequality*), Rousseau grants that savages, while better than most civilized men, are often murderous and cruel. The reason is that *even* savages live in *societies*, many of which are corrupt, and therefore, they are well removed from natural or pre-social man.[26] It is, then, only pre-social man that is wholly good or perfect. Rousseau also grants that natural man may be merely an intellectual construct, a conceptual experiment to discover God's man, man unmarred by his own works.[27] Indeed, when we envisage natural man, we find that being pre-social he is pre-human for he lacks language and reason.[28] Still, the conceptual experiment is necessary in that only when we have distilled God's man can we discover a criterion of good, distinguish man's natural or instinctive passions from those which society's conventions have engendered. For despite being pre-human, natural man is a perfect animal, characterized by the instincts of self-preservation and compassion for others.[29] Rousseau compares him to civilized man who, in becoming human, often becomes a 'depraved animal', a creature that is weak, cowardly, and servile.[30] The word 'often' needs to be stressed, for even as early as the second Discourse, Rousseau hints that civilized society need not be corrupting if only we could eliminate those aspects of it that subordinate the weak to the powerful.[31] Then, and only then, we might be able to bring the conventions of society into accord with nature.

In sum, a comparison of the first and second Discourses discloses that Rousseau's position has altered in two ways. First, he has replaced his dichotomy between savage and civilized man with a distinction between pre-social and socialized man. Having done this, he uses his new distinction to suggest a *new sort* of ethical distinction. In the old dichotomy, savage was equated with good and civilized with evil, two mutually exclusive terms. In the new distinction, pre-social is equated with the natural and social with the conventional, which is a *very different thing* in that while what is pre-social or natural now serves Rousseau as a criterion of good, what is social or conventional is not necessarily evil. For conventions may be either good or evil, depending on whether they are in accord with nature. Second, Rousseau has begun to do something that I have not commented on until now, that is, he has begun to apologize *even for* pre-social man! For example, he concedes that natural man will at times take hasty revenge and that he might seize the food or dwelling of another.[32] He tries to dismiss these seemingly vicious or selfish tendencies by calling attention to pre-social man's pre-human character. Natural man cannot even recognize others as his fellow-men and therefore, will feel no sense of injustice when harmed by another; rather, it will seem no different from being bitten by an animal or hurt by a stone, no different from a pain that demands relief rather than revenge.[33] This last point will assume importance when we begin to criticize Rousseau.

Rousseau's plans for social reform, which are merely implicit in the second Discourse, reach maturity in his later works. In the *Emile*, civilized society's illness is diagnosed. It corrupts man only in so far as it forces one man to bow to the will of another. If Emile breaks the windows in his room, you must not force him to obey you. Leave the windows unfixed and when he feels winter's cold, he will feel punished not by man but by the impersonal change of the seasons.[34] In the *Social Contract*, Rousseau finds the cure for society's ills in that product of the social contract, the general will. We cannot here take time to explore the nature of the general will, but it can serve as a cure for several reasons: it entails submitting only to laws which one feels should be obeyed impartially by all men, so in a sense one submits, not to others, but to oneself; it is an abstract principle, so submitting to it is submitting to something as impersonal as a physical law, e.g. the law of gravity; and finally, the general will is infallible, so submitting to it is submitting to something as unchallengeable as a physical law. Thus reformed, society need not corrupt man by enslaving him. Thus freed from the degrading influence of submission to others, man can live in accord with his instinct of compassion for his fellow-men.

*   *   *

It is now time to state the critique of modern natural right that I find convincing, a critique that draws heavily on Tawney and Mill.

Mill begins his examination of those who would base ethics on the concept of nature by drawing a distinction between *defining* the word 'good' and offering a *criterion* of good and evil. He assumes that the proponents of the doctrine of modern natural right are not doing the former, that is, he cannot believe they merely mean that when we call something 'good', we could just as easily call it 'in accord with nature'. Such an assertion would be a merely verbal proposition, such as saying that the words 'car' and 'horse-less-carriage' are interchangeable.[35] Mill seems to be correct in his assumption. Locke and Rousseau attempted to envisage natural man, not so they could define the word 'good', but so they could discover a criterion of good and evil.

Therefore, Mill proceeds to criticize the statement, 'what is in accord with nature is right', as a criterion of good. He mounts a devastating critique of those who apply such a test simplistically. If by nature they mean the whole physical universe including its physical laws, then *everything* man does is good; a suicide who jumps off a cliff is obeying the law of gravity as much as a man strolling down the street. If by nature they mean the universe uninfluenced by man's behaviour, then *everything* man does is bad, for even breathing influences the content of the earth's atmosphere. Thus, such devotees of nature are left with *no* workable criterion to distinguish good from evil.[36] And while such men may seem to be men of straw, in fact one finds them everywhere. Everything from lightning-rods to organ transplants have been condemned as an unwarranted human interference with the course of nature.

However, Mill is quite aware that this critique will not satisfy the advocates of modern natural right. For Locke and Rousseau, unlike the above simplistic types, did not focus on untouched man or nature because they thought that the world should be left unaltered. Rather, they hoped to find there a datum which they could use to discover purposes or values that ought to guide human conduct. Against the Lockean notion of looking for God's design in the untouched world of physical nature, Mill emphasizes the unlovely aspects of nature, nature 'red in tooth and claw' cruelly destroying life by plague, storm, famine, and disaster.[37] The implication is that such thinkers do not really survey nature untouched by man to develop a criterion of good and evil but rather, pick and choose within that realm according to their own predilections.[38] And it is difficult to fault Mill on this point, particularly when we reflect on the details of Locke's derivation of human rights. When Locke uses the natural equality of men to argue that men have a right to consent to their rulers, we feel that he could have just as easily argued that the hereditary differences between men, the fact that some are born with greater intelligence or talent, mean that some men are born to exploit others. In sum, Locke does not *derive* a criterion of good from nature untouched by man ; he has a *preconceived* humane criterion which he uses to judge nature !

As for Rousseau's version of natural right, Mill launches the usual attack on the benevolence of savages, something which would not have troubled the Rousseau of the second Discourse as we have seen. But he also attacks Rousseau's pre-social or instinctive man. Mill points out the obvious, namely, that almost every virtue we can think of is the result of taming our instincts rather than following them. For example : courage comes from conquering fear, which is instinctive ; cleanliness represents a triumph over our natural fondness for dirt ; if sympathy is natural, it extends only to our immediate circle and is accompanied by callousness to 'outsiders'.[39] In order to reinforce Mill's critique, I would like to remind you of Rousseau's attempt to explain away the vicious tendencies of pre-social man, his 'seeming' pugnacity and selfishness. Rousseau tells us that pre-social man is pre-human and that therefore, we can discount these tendencies because they are not truly analogous to human vices, are not really like cruelty and selfishness. But this makes it obvious that Rousseau is playing a double game. He has no objection to our considering the benevolent tendencies of pre-social man as models for human virtues. If natural man's vices are to be discounted because of his pre-human character, why not his virtues? Like Locke, Rousseau has a preconceived humane criterion that he uses to assess the pre-social man from whom his criterion of good is supposed to be derived.

We can now appreciate the magnitude of the failure of modern natural right. It was meant to perform the humane task of providing a basis for human rights, so as to protect men from exploitation. Yet, when we apply fairly the tests for good and evil suggested by Locke and Rousseau, we arrive at non-humane results. Their criteria just do not correlate with humane criteria. Both Locke and Rousseau sense this and therefore, are driven to utilize implicit humane criteria to assess their explicit criteria whenever the latter threaten to produce vicious results.

After Mill, Tawney took up the task of devastating the doctrine of modern natural right. Tawney gave Mill's argument a new twist. Mill had shown that the criteria suggested by modern natural right were not equivalent to a humane criterion of *good*; Tawney shows that they are not equivalent to a humane criterion of *justice*. He argues along these lines: The core of the doctrine of natural right is that the individual is born with certain rights and that these rights are pre-social, exist anterior to the society in which they function.[40] Using this premiss, Locke and Rousseau argued that certain rights of the individual were inalienable or absolute, that they were unalterable and did not have to be justified in terms of any social purpose.[41] Tawney believes that such a doctrine tends to allow rights to become privileges; for example, take the notion that the owner of property should be allowed the whole of the profits there-from. In pre-industrial England, this right could be justified in so far as certain social conditions prevailed, that is, in so far as men owned the farms or tools they worked, it guaranteed to the worker the fruits of his labour. But with the rise of industrialism, such a right meant that the idle capitalist investor, the legal owner of the industrial plant, reaped the lion's share of the profit.[42] Since property rights were thought to be absolute and to require no social justification, the right remained unchanged while society altered. What once had a social purpose and therefore was properly a *right* became socially dysfunctional and therefore, a *privilege*. For the very definition of a privilege is a right that cannot be justified in social terms, in terms of how it functions within society.[43] In sum, the notion that the individual possesses pre-social or absolute rights leads to privilege and therefore, *injustice*.

Tawney applied this analysis only to property rights but actually, it can be applied to all rights. For every right, as Tawney sees, is really a *power* that is guaranteed by law; and *all power* must be justified in terms of social utility or it becomes absolute power and therefore, dangerous.[44] Even the right of free speech is a legalized opportunity to influence the opinions of others, indeed, one may succeed in revolutionizing society. Governments are only too aware of this, which is why they attempt to restrict 'free speech' to situations in which debate cannot influence events. The potency of free speech is one reason why Mill felt that his famous justification of it, *On Liberty*, had to include a justification in terms of social utility. The implications of Tawney's thesis, that all of the rights of the individual are powers and must be justified in terms of social utility, may seem dangerous. But note how triumphantly Mill succeeds in his task. And note that Tawney also applies his thesis to the powers of the state: we have a right to ask for a social justification for *every power* which government claims as its own.[45]

That the powers of the state and the rights of the individual must be assessed in a social context would have appealed to both Plato and Aristotle. They too reject as artificial the approach of those who, like Locke and Rousseau, would attempt to base political ethics on a pre-social foundation ; indeed, they take it as self-evident that we can derive adequate criteria only by viewing man in the context of a perfected human society. But Tawney's thesis has an interest for us that goes beyond this. If he is correct, rights can be justified only in the context of a certain society and its way of life. Which means that the problem of justifying a certain set of human rights is seen to be a facet of a larger problem, namely, *how to justify the way of life that lends those rights justification*. For example, if we turn to the U.S. Bill of Rights, we are assessing something that is functional only in the context of a certain sort of society, a society that stresses humane values and spontaneity rather than coercion. Thus, to justify something like the Bill of Rights we must find a way of justifying a humane-libertarian way of life. Which means, as we have seen, that we must find a way of showing that such a life has objective or non-partisan validity —that it is somehow valid for those who do not at present appreciate it as well as for those who do.

And this last suggests a final flaw in the doctrine of modern natural right, *perhaps the most significant flaw that it contains*. Even if Locke and Rousseau had succeeded in deriving humane criteria of justice and goodness, where in their works is the *justification* of humane criteria *vis-à-vis* an opponent who espouses fundamentally non-humane values? These thinkers seem merely to *assume* that what is natural in the sense of pre-social has objective or non-partisan validity. Or better, they offer little more than a brief theological justification, a few paragraphs which argue that nature untouched by man is the work of God and therefore, must be objectively good. Of this justification, I will only say that it raises grave philosophical problems and involves religious beliefs largely rejected in our own time.

*　　*　　*

If I am to escape the charge that my account of the approach and defects of modern natural right is a gross over-simplification, some elaboration is needed. First, the reader must be careful to distinguish the *means* a thinker deems necessary for the perfection of men from his *method* of gaining ethical truth. There is no doubt that Locke and Rousseau, at least the later Rousseau (recall that he came to grant that pre-social man was pre-human), emphasize that society is a necessary means to making men fully human. Indeed, they emphasize this just as much as Plato and Aristotle and we can find passage after passage in their works which could easily have been written by the ancients. But when Locke and Rousseau ask what sort of society makes men fully human, when they search for a criterion for assessing various societies and the sort of man they produce, then they *do use* the distinction between *pre-social* and *social* man as a method of discovering a criterion of good and evil, or better, as a method of distinguishing the natural from the conventional. In a word : Locke would have us turn to the laws of nature he derives from viewing physical nature (including pre-social man) as it comes from the hand of God and ask whether our society obeys those laws ; Rousseau would have us turn to natural or pre-social man and ask whether our society encourages his virtues to flower and avoids inculcating the slavish vices he lacks. Again, to drive the point home, I do not claim that Locke or the later Rousseau hold that men can achieve perfection in a pre-social state. I merely claim that the intellectual construct of a pre-social state is central to their method of gaining ethical truth.

However, this defence of my analysis raises a second point. Even if we confine ourselves to the epistemological methods of Locke and Rousseau, my account might be attacked on the grounds that it gives too little weight to their later writings. For example, there is a case to be made that the Rousseau of the *Social Contract* does not use the general will merely as a means of reforming society, as a means of eliminating the master–slave relationships which encourage slavish vices ; rather, at times at least, he seems to adopt it as a method of gaining ethical truth. He tells us that a rule or law is in accord with the general will if each member of society, when thinking impartially rather than in terms of private or partisan interests, is willing to see it applied to all. Many have noted the resemblance between this and Kant's test of what is truly moral ; namely, can we will that a maxim should become a universal law?

Note the following statement in the *Social Contract* :[46]

> The passage from the state of nature to the civil state produces a very remarkable change in man, by substituting justice for instinct in his conduct, and giving his actions the morality they had formerly lacked. Then only, when the voice of duty takes the place of physical impulses and right of appetite, does man, who so far had considered only himself, find that he is forced to act on different principles, and to consult his reason before listening to his inclinations.

And a bit later Rousseau tells us that 'the mere impulse of appetite is slavery, while obedience to a law which we prescribe to ourselves is liberty'.[47] These passages seem almost to anticipate Mill's critique of the early Rousseau ; they seem to downgrade the search for man's natural desires, his pre-social instincts, as a method for determining good and evil in favour of consulting 'reason', the latter perhaps referring to the general will. Note particularly the reference to obeying 'a law which we prescribe to ourselves', which seems to be a short-hand statement of the principle of the general will.

It is, then, quite arguable that while the *Social Contract* continues to give a nod to natural or pre-social man as indicative of what traits a good society should foster, Rousseau really abandons him in favour of a proto-Kantian road to ethical truth, that is, the general will takes over as the method Rousseau uses to justify certain value criteria and attack others. Some scholars have proposed a similar thesis in regard to Locke's later work. They argue that while the *Second Treatise* indeed continues to cite the laws of nature, Locke places more emphasis on enlightened self-interest as a rationale against unlimited state power, that is, he attacks Hobbes primarily in terms of prudence rather than principle. This is held to indicate that Locke had lost confidence in the method of gaining ethical truth formulated in his early writings. I have many more reservations about this sort of thesis in regard to Locke than Rousseau, but I am not overly concerned to refute it. For what does this thesis mean? It means that Locke and Rousseau lost faith in the distinctive epistemological method of modern natural right, lost faith to the point of leaving the ranks of natural right thinkers entirely in order to espouse Kantianism or enlightened self-interest. What better evidence of the defects of the natural right approach to ethical truth could we have, than that its brilliant pioneers found it wanting? As far as this work is concerned, it is the philosophical problem of the merits of this approach, not interpretative problems about Locke and Rousseau, that is central. My purpose is not to show that Locke and Rousseau never abandoned this approach, but rather to give the reader cause to abandon it.

To sum up, I am convinced of the following: Hobbes's world of sense and desire was the *starting point* for Locke and Rousseau; their early methods of deriving ethical truth are properly called natural right approaches, for they are based on distinguishing the natural from the conventional; Rousseau probably and Locke possibly abandoned their early epistemological methods in their later works; however, it makes no sense to call the approaches they may have substituted, whether proto-Kantian or enlightened self-interest, natural right approaches; therefore, if they did abandon the epistemological method of modern natural right, this merely underscores its vulnerability.

Actually, what impresses one most about the distinctive epistemological method of natural right *is* its vulnerability to critique. But now that we understand the source of that vulnerability, we can sympathize with the founders of modern natural right. Hobbes set them an impossible task.

He appalled them by his scepticism and thus, they felt the need to salvage the distinction between the natural and the conventional. However, he also trapped them in his own phenomenal world and thus, they attempted to transfer the classical distinction, which had been based on the doctrine of essences, to a realm of sense and desire. Plato and Aristotle would have reinforced our sympathy with their own. They would have anticipated the tortuous struggles of anyone who thought that their distinction could be transplanted to such alien soil. This is not to say that the ancients thought that ethics should ignore the realm of sense and desire. Recall that this realm, the realm of becoming, the actual world, was *part* of their four-fold phenomenal universe. Plato held that one must pass through it as one ascended the divided line to the world of Forms or Essences. Aristotle went further and focused on it, focused on actual men and societies caught in the act of living. However, even Aristotle held that one must view human history through the spectacles of the doctrine of essences, that the latter was a necessary part of one's conceptual equipment. And both of the ancients agreed that anyone who depended *solely* on sense and desire as the key to ethical truth was doomed to failure. Most of the critique levelled by Mill and Tawney could just as easily have come from the ancients themselves.

All of this suggests that it is time to throw off the legacy of Hobbes. If the attempt to transplant the classical distinction between the natural and the conventional has proved fruitless, we might do well to restore it to its original soil. It is, then, worth exploring a return to classical natural law. But again, we will not aim at restoring the doctrine of essences as a metaphysics. Rather, we will hope to discover *concepts* that will allow us to deal with the problem of scepticism, the problem of objective or non-partisan validity, *concepts* that will allow us to assess man's experience with different ways of life in terms of which of them best realizes the potentialities of his essence or nature.

NOTES

1 *Universal Declaration of Human Rights*, U.N. Doc. A/811, 16 Dec. 1948.

2 Staughton Lynd, *Intellectual Origins of American Radicalism* (London: Faber & Faber, 1969).

3 Thomas Hobbes, *Leviathan* in *The English Works of Thomas Hobbes*, ed. W. Molesworth (London: John Bohn, 1839), Vol. III, p. 21.

4 *Ibid.*, pp. 672–4.

5 *Ibid.*, pp. 672–6.

6 *Ibid.*, p. 664.

7 *Ibid.*, p. 669.

8 *Ibid.*, p. 41.

9 *Ibid.*, p. 669.

10 *Ibid.*, pp. 682–3.

11 *Ibid.*, p. 190.

12 *Ibid.*, p. 120.

13 *Ibid.*, pp. 204–6.

14 John Locke, *Essays on the Law of Nature*, ed. W. von Leyden (London: Oxford University Press, 1954), pp. 139, 141.

15 *Ibid.*, p. 133.

16 *Ibid.*, p. 157.

17 *Ibid.*, pp. 77–82.

18 John Locke, *First Treatise on Civil Government*, Section 137.

19 Jean-Jacques Rousseau, *Emile* (London: Dent, 1911), pp. 249–50.

20 Locke, *Essays on the Law of Nature*, pp. 157, 159, 195.

21 John Locke, *Second Treatise on Civil Government*, Section 6.

22 Locke, *First Treatise*, Section 67; also see the *Second Treatise*, Section 4.

23 Locke, *Second Treatise*, Section 23.

24 *Ibid.*, Sections 26, 27, 45.

25 Jean-Jacques Rousseau, *Discourse on the Arts and Sciences* in the Everyman edition of *The Social Contract and Discourses* (London: Dent, 1913), pp. 132–5, 142. All citations of the *Discourses* and the *Social Contract* refer to the Everyman edition.

26 Jean-Jacques Rousseau, *Discourse on the Origin of Inequality*, pp. 212–14.

27 *Ibid.*, pp. 168–70.

28 *Ibid.*, p. 203.

29 *Ibid.*, pp. 171–2.

30 *Ibid.*, pp. 181–2.

31 *Ibid.*, pp. 173, 205.

32 *Ibid.*, pp. 200, 204–5.

33 *Ibid.*, pp. 200, 197.

34 Rousseau, *Emile*, pp. 49, 64.

35 John Stuart Mill, *Three Essays on Religion* (London: Longmans, 1874), pp. 12–13.

36 *Ibid.*, pp. 15–20.

37 *Ibid.*, pp. 28–31.

38 *Ibid.*, pp. 23–4.

39 *Ibid.*, pp. 43–52.

40 R. H. Tawney, *The Acquisitive Society* (New York: Harvest Books, 1955), pp. 20–2.

41 *Ibid.*, pp. 13–15.

42 *Ibid.*, pp. 56–62.

43 *Ibid.*, p. 24.

44 *Ibid.*, p. 50.

45 *Ibid.*, p. 51.

46 Jean-Jacques Rousseau, *Social Contract* (see note 25 of this chapter), p. 18.

47 *Ibid.*, p. 19.

5

Aristotle and the Status of Ideological Appeals

The preliminaries are over. I have tried to convince the reader that the problem of ethical truth versus scepticism is important, that ethical scepticism is not to be welcomed, and that natural law does not stand or fall with the doctrine of modern natural right. Hopefully, he is now prepared to give a neo-Aristotelian approach to the above problem a fair hearing.

We must, then, come directly to grips with the central question which dominates this work : can it be shown that ideological appeals on behalf of a certain way of life have non-rhetorical significance? Can it be shown that it makes sense to claim that a certain way of life has objective or non-partisan validity, that it is somehow best for mankind, not merely for those men who happen to value it? Although I am convinced that a neo-Aristotelian approach will provide the key to answering this question, I wish to deliver a warning in advance : that such an approach focuses on one form of goodness, namely eudemonic goodness (happiness or felicity), as more promising than other forms (most notably, moral goodness) in terms of making a case for objective or non-partisan status ; and further, that this in itself can engender certain problems.

This chapter will evidence a shift of emphasis in references to the way of life that I obviously have in mind as the most promising candidate for objective or non-partisan status.

From here on, references will be to what I have called the 'humanist ideal', the life of humane love and creative work, rather than to the 'Jeffersonian ideal', the humane-libertarian way of life. I admit to a preference for the Jeffersonian ideal : its emphasis on comradeship, humane involvement, creative work and leisure, artistic and scientific experimentation, and freedom from arbitrary coercion seems to me to embody the highest expression of humanism. However, we used the debate between Jeffersonians and conservative Social Darwinists in America primarily as an illustration, that is, we used it to provide a concrete example of humane men whose *esprit de corps* was threatened by the problem of ethical scepticism. And I do not intend to allow an illustration to trap me into attempting to justify the Jeffersonian ideal against those who espouse other versions of humanism. This would involve me in a different, and much more difficult, chore than the task undertaken in this work, the task of justifying humanism against its ideological opponents. The reader will also notice a shift in the sort of ideologue envisioned as our non-humane opponent. As we leave the American scene, just as the humanist ideal will replace Jeffersonianism, a democratized version of humanism, so the Nietzschean will replace the Social Darwinist, a democratized sort of 'Nietzschean' one finds in America.

Thanks to my empirical approach to ethical truth, the justification offered on behalf of the humanist ideal will be based on evidence, on an analysis of what men have discovered about themselves as they have lived various ways of life. This means, of course, that I will have to state my conclusions in a tentative way, to say only that, according to my assessment, the evidence thus far favours a certain way of life rather than its competitors. The reader should keep in mind that I am a partisan of the ideal selected as the most promising, that the emotional impetus behind my work derives largely from the hope of justifying the humanist ideal, and that therefore, he would do well to approach my assessment of the evidence in a critical frame of mind.

In effect, the remainder of this work will attempt the

following : (1) To show that one *can* legitimately claim that a certain way of life possesses non-partisan validity, or better, that one can do this without saying anything that is *philosophically* (as distinct from empirically) indefensible—a task undertaken in this chapter ; (2) to qualify this contention by emphasizing that such claims are defensible only if they are made in terms of eudemonic goodness (happiness) rather than moral goodness—also included in this chapter ; (3) to defend my neo-Aristotelian approach, a 'naturalistic' approach based on the distinction between the natural and the conventional, against the 'naturalistic fallacy', the chief objection usually raised against it—Chapter 6 ; (4) to explore a difficulty posed by our inability to make a case that a certain way of life has non-partisan validity in terms of moral goodness, a difficulty I have called 'the problem of the moral hero'—Chapter 7.

*   *   *

The above statement of my second and fourth tasks reflects the fact that I have been influenced by G. H. von Wright, a thinker who emphasizes the necessity of distinguishing a variety of forms of goodness, a variety of ways in which men judge things to be good. Indeed, throughout this work, particularly when clarifying the nature of ethical scepticism, I have implied that there are important differences between various kinds of goodness. It is interesting to note that the ancients distinguished certain forms of goodness, namely, those most relevant to ethics, eudemonic (happiness), hedonic (pleasure), and moral goodness ; however, they tended to make the mistake of attempting to elevate one of these forms to a position of the highest good. Von Wright, who like myself draws heavily on the ancients, not only goes on to distinguish carefully many other forms of goodness but also goes beyond any previous thinker in illuminating the philosophical significance of the fact that there are many varieties of goodness, as we shall see when we begin to deal with the question of the naturalistic fallacy.

Let me, then, offer a brief description of the varieties of goodness that von Wright discusses: (1) Instrumental goodness—when we say that something, perhaps an arte-fact, is good of its kind, e.g. when we say a knife is good for the purpose of a knife, that is, cutting; (2) technical good-ness—this refers to those who are skilled at some activity or art, either one like chess-playing that provides its own criterion of excellence (winning) or one like doctoring that is done well in so far as it is an effective instrument for social purposes; (3) utilitarian goodness—a thing or activity is useful when it can be used to achieve some end, e.g. a broken knife might be useful as a door-stop even though it is no good as a knife; (4) medical goodness—the good of an organ (e.g. the heart) or a mental faculty (e.g. the memory) that is functioning properly (pumping blood or allowing one to remember things), and includes the good of living beings that feel fit, not merely physically but psychologically as well, among which the good of a man, a man whose life flowers into well-being or happiness, falls by analogy; (5) the beneficial—a thing or activity that favourably affects the good of a being and thus, it is a special case of utilitarian goodness; (6) hedonic goodness—a good taste or apple or holiday, good in the sense of pleasant; (7) eudemonic goodness—the attitude towards one's life that prompts the judgment 'I am happy', which judgment differs from hedonic judgments in constituting an assessment of one's life as a whole rather than merely some particular event; (8) moral goodness—'an act is morally good, if and only if it does good to at least one being and does not do bad (harm) to any being'.[1]

Von Wright emphasizes that his discussion is not exhaus-tive, that there are many uses of 'good' difficult to classify neatly, e.g. 'good manners', 'good as gold', 'a good book', etc.[2] This is not to imply, however, that these uses are mysterious or somehow not subject to analysis.

At this point, I must part company with von Wright, although I will acknowledge another debt later on. Unfor-tunately, we differ precisely on those forms of goodness that are of greatest interest to political ethics, that is, on the nature of happiness or eudemonic goodness (which seems to him merely an attitude[3] but to me a pattern of experience that 'includes' an attitude) and the nature of moral goodness (which seems to him a form only in a secondary sense, if at all,[4] but to me a form in its own right—a difference that prompts me to think of his definition of moral goodness quoted above as merely a humane criterion of moral behaviour). Moreover, I fear that my approach to the central problem of political ethics, that is, whether or not some way of life can be said to possess objective or non-partisan validity, is eccentric and therefore shared by no one else.

Perhaps contrasting pleasure and happiness will provide a good starting point for clarifying the nature of the latter. Pleasure presents a problem in that men speak of pleasures in a variety of ways, some of which are more inclusive than others. We all find certain experiences satisfying in the sense of delectable or thrilling or satiating. But sometimes men use 'pleasure' to refer to nothing save satisfactions of desire, that is, sensual pleasures plus the satisfaction of egocentric lusts, e.g. the lust for power. At other times, they include 'higher' satisfactions, such as aesthetic enjoyment, or even all human fulfilling experiences except moral ones, the sense of living a noble life. The broadest use of pleasure includes literally all human fulfilments; however, even here pleasure can be distinguished from happiness. For, as noted above, we call experiences pleasant as they occur one by one. While we say that we are happy only if we find life fulfilling taken as a whole, only if we enjoy a life characterized by a pattern of broad, vivid, and harmonious fulfilling experience. It is because happiness has to do with a summary judgment passed on one's whole way of life that men place happiness ahead of pleasure, feel that it is more important to be happy than to enjoy certain pleasures; and this in turn explains why philosophers, e.g. the utilitarians, who advise us to live so as to maximize pleasure usually end up, like John Stuart Mill, so expanding the meaning of pleasure as to make it a synonym of happiness.

There is another point about happiness that calls for clarification right at the start. Note that I have said that happiness consists of a pattern of *broad*, *vivid*, and *harmonious* fulfilling experience. All three of these terms need elaboration, but for the moment I want to focus on harmony, what the ancients called 'harmony of soul' and what we might call 'peace of mind' or 'a sense of well-being' or 'the feeling that life is good'. What these phrases imply, I think, is that happiness is more than variegated (broad) and intense (vivid) fulfilling experiences, for these after all fill only a small part of our lives. In between times, if a man suffers from tension, feels at war with himself, his happiness is diminished. The happy man enjoys a consistent aura of well-being, his specific fulfilling experiences take place against a background of emotional harmony; ideally, they are crescendos that rise out of a consistent refrain that sings 'life is good', albeit a refrain often so soft it escapes our attention. Aristotle once compared happiness to a necklace. Appropriating his analogy, we might say that a harmonious emotional world is the thread on which the beads of fulfilling experience are strung, never forgetting, of course, that there must be lustrous beads to string or happiness would be incomplete. For our intense fulfilments, e.g. experiencing a sense of achievement, proclaim the same message as the emotional harmony that connects them; built into their very texture is the inarticulate 'judgment' that life (for the moment at least) is good. And they serve to raise the volume of this message to a point where it is fully audible.

Now, if someone wishes to call this persistent thread that runs through the happy man's emotional world an 'attitude' towards his life, I have no real objection, so long as it is granted that it is an experienced or felt attitude rather than an *adopted* one. Men possess many attitudes that are experienced, attitudes such as excitement, anger, love, hate, etc. Certainly, when we are thrilled by someone or are angry at someone, we have a certain attitude towards them and yet, these are things we experience. That happiness is experienced is obscured because it is not a discrete emotion like a thrill or anger, but consists of a pattern of emotion experienced over many years. Yet, love and hate are also patterns which may persist over many years. And note that the experienced attitudes listed, anger, love, etc., are not ones we adopt; often we do not know that we possess them until we are overwhelmed by feelings of anger or love.

The man who has suffered through a period of misery will understand this distinction. His life (or his personality) alters, he goes from misery through a sense of contentment towards positive enjoyment of life, and one day he realizes that he is happy. It is not that *he* has passed judgment on the changed pattern and tenor of his emotional world; rather, the new tenor of his experience has passed a 'judgment' on his life *for him*. He has a new attitude towards life, if you will, but he has not adopted this attitude—it has adopted him.

This inarticulate 'judgment' that happiness passes on our lives makes me dissatisfied with calling happiness a pattern of experience, a phrase that seems too non-specific. The word 'judgment' is also awkward, for we often use it in the sense of a formal, articulate judgment, stating an opinion about something after due consideration. Perhaps it would be best to call happiness a 'finding' in that happiness consists of a pattern of experience in which one *finds* life (eudemonically) good, rather like the experience of finding oneself thrilled by a concert. Or perhaps an even better word would be 'realization', for happiness is not a sudden or abrupt realization as when we find ourselves thrilled, but rather a gradual, continuous, cumulative realization or awareness of a heightened quality in life. To borrow a book title it is a 'gradual joy'. In sum, happiness is a finding or realization in two ways: one finds that one is happy and *in* finding that one is happy, one *finds life good*, good in a certain sense, of course, fulfilling or eudemonically good (as distinct from morally good). For a man can be happy and yet believe that he is morally remiss; the two are logically compatible at least, although psychologically the latter belief may undermine his happiness.

We have said that happiness consists of *broad* and *vivid* fulfilling experiences and a *harmonious* emotional world. It is now time to clarify these three terms by way of concrete examples. The examples are drawn from Ruth Benedict's *Patterns of Culture* ;[5] they are used merely as illustrations in that anthropologists today agree that Benedict committed errors of fact and interpretation.

The Zunis, a Pueblo Indian people of the U.S. southwest, emphasize harmony of soul to an unusual degree. Their whole way of life is founded on the assumption of a natural harmony within man, between men, and between man and nature, that is, the gods. They channel most of their emotional energy into a temperate ceremonial religion whose prayers are always pleas for peace and security. Their way of life produces a mildly happy sort of man, who is calm, sociable, co-operative, whose emotional life has a pleasant, steady tenor. However, the extreme harmony characteristic of their emotional world is bought at some sacrifice of breadth ; Zunis miss out on such fulfilments as those of individual achievement or triumphing over great odds. The sacrifice in vividness of fulfilment is even greater ; the blandness of their emotional life leaves no room for strong feelings of any sort, for example, they enjoy no intense love relationships. On the other hand, the Kwakiutls, who once flourished on Vancouver Island, were men of a very different sort, a people of tremendous zest and verve whose fulfilments were vivid indeed. They were almost totally engrossed in a competition, revolving around the acquisition and display of wealth, designed to shame one's opponent and afford oneself the delights of triumph and self-glorification. A Kwakiutl would choose his wife, not because of affection or suitability for child-rearing, but to gain an opportunity to engage her father in a display competition. In effect, their whole emotional world was limited to the narrow arc between triumph and shame. They sacrificed not only breadth of fulfilment but also emotional harmony. Since they staked everything on a grandiose picture of themselves, any loss or defeat was likely to bring demoralization or suicide. And defeats inevitably came, for even natural deaths were looked upon as defeats inflicted by the gods.

It is hard to find examples of whole peoples who have given up vividness of fulfilment and harmony in favour of mere breadth of fulfilment. We might do well, therefore, to look at those members of our own society who have been trapped by a consumer-oriented culture into a continual scramble for the new and novel in possessions and pleasures, a scramble that has robbed them of both harmony of soul and the intense satisfactions of love and creative work. Focusing on them seems appropriate in that our examples have been chosen to illustrate not only the three 'factors' which make up happiness but also that these three are functionally interrelated. Probably the very act of isolating these factors distorts happiness as a phenomenon, but it seems better to do it some violence than to leave it entirely unanalysed.

Having distinguished happiness from pleasure, we must now briefly distinguish moral goodness from happiness. Men do not stop at finding certain experiences exciting, or at finding their way of life fulfilling; they judge certain actions to be either morally admirable or morally repugnant.

In my opinion, G. E. Moore came the closest to catching the nature of moral goodness when he emphasized that we sometimes say that certain things are *intrinsically good*, that they *ought to exist*.[6] For when I say that a certain action is morally good, this is equivalent to saying that I *ought* to do it *whether I want to or not*!* Moral propositions are really comparison of value propositions of a peculiar sort, propositions which say that something has a value *qualitatively superior* to hedonic or eudemonic goodness. Or better, when we judge an action to have moral or intrinsic value, we judge it valuable in a way which makes whether or not we (as distinct from others) find pleasure in that action seem

---

* The equivalence holds, of course, only if I am the *sort of person* capable of the action. For example, I might think it morally good to perform a dangerous mission; but if I lack heroism, and if anyone but a hero would lose his nerve and botch the mission, I would do well not to undertake it.

irrelevant. We can see this clearly if we recall times when what we judged to be morally good was in direct conflict with hedonic or eudemonic goodness, times when we very much wanted to do an action, were strongly tempted by it, but also felt that we ought not to do it *however much* we wanted to. I use the word 'felt' with intention, in that man is such that his emotions can be moulded so as to take on a moral texture. Parents, educators, and governments recognize this and train us from childhood to feel moral revulsion towards tempting anti-social behaviour, e.g. taking advantage of others. And most of us, I hope, feel an over-powering emotion of 'this should not be' when we dwell on certain actions, let us say read the diary of Anne Frank and dwell on the senseless murder of this young girl and millions of others by the Nazis.

As we have seen, Plato was fully aware of the above function of moral feelings and therefore, was probably also aware of the nature of moral judgments. This emerges most clearly in his analysis of man's soul into reason, spirit or moral indignation, and the passions. Reason may judge what a man ought to do, but cool reason needs an ally against the powerful emotive force exerted by tempting pleasures; therefore, it trains spirit or moral indignation to approve what reason recommends, thereby enlisting an emotive ally to counteract the force of pleasure.[7] Plato dramatizes his point with a brilliant analogy in the *Phaedrus*, where he compares man's soul to a chariot, the driver representing reason, the noble horse spirit, and the wayward horse the passions;[8] the driver trains the lead horse to follow his directions so as to bring the wayward horse into line. In other words, what Moore stated explicitly is implicit in Plato, that moral judgments and moral feelings stamp a thing as intrinsically good, good in a way which discounts pleasure as irrelevant. Moreover, this view of moral judgments tallies nicely with the rule of universalizability, the contention that universalizing our moral assessments is one of their defining characteristics: to say that an action is *intrinsically good* (in certain circumstances) entails assessing it to be good (in those circumstances) no matter who does it.

I hope the reader sees that this account of moral goodness is consistent with the position taken earlier in this work, that is, the above does *not* imply that moral assessments include a claim to objective status. We must not confuse three distinct things: the tension between moral goodness and the passions; universalizability; a claim to objective status. The first two refer to *my* assessments, to what *I* put ahead of my desires and whether *I* praise others for acts for which I praise myself. The third refers to a situation in which someone rejects my assessments, in which someone says that he puts other things ahead of his desires and that he applies some other moral criterion consistently. The third involves a claim that my assessments are worthy of regard from *someone else* even though he does not share them. However, having said this, I wish to remind the reader that whether moral assessments are inclusive of a claim to objective status is not crucial. Even if this were so, it would not, in my opinion, save us the trouble of attempting to make a case in support of such a claim.

Most of the forms of goodness cannot be utilized in any serious attempt to show that a certain way of life has objective or non-partisan validity; they do not represent ways in which men assess their way of life but have to do with evaluating mere artefacts or fragments of a way of life, things such as knives or treating the sick. In their attempts to deal with the problem of objectivity, philosophers have, therefore, usually turned to eudemonic, hedonic, or moral goodness. I will not attempt to utilize the latter two forms because I feel that they are unpromising options, what with the failures of Kant (who turned to the nature of moral judg-ment) and the utilitarians (who used hedonic good to argue in favour of a humane life—promoting the greatest good of the greatest number). I will not present my own criticisms of these thinkers, but will merely say that I accept the modern critique of Kant, that while men must universalize their moral judgments no one moral code is uniquely universalizable (look back to Chapter 1), and G. E. Moore's critique of Mill, at least when it is reformulated (as it can be) to avoid confused references to the 'naturalistic fallacy'.

*   *   *

How, then, can we make a case that a certain way of life possesses objective or non-partisan validity in terms of *eudemonic goodness*? I will begin by stating a concept of good shared by both Plato[9] and Aristotle,[10] namely: there is a state for man analogous to overall health. However, my development of this concept will proceed along fundamentally Aristotelian lines.

Note that the above is called a 'concept' rather than a definition or even a proposition. For, despite appearances, it is really not a proposition at all, but rather a germinal concept, something that lays the foundations for a conceptual system made up of at least three propositions (some of whose terms, e.g. happiness, require careful definition, as we have seen). The best way to reveal the three propositions hidden in the above concept is to ask why Aristotle accepted it. Aristotle was convinced that just as a really healthy body (the body of a man in good shape—not merely a body free of disease) gives rise to a sense of *physical* well-being, so when man's whole nature, mind and body, is functioning in a certain way (living in a way characterized by virtue), man enjoys maximum happiness or felicity as a natural result. Therefore, it is legitimate to say that there is a state for (the whole) man analogous to health ; a man in that state maximizes his sense of *psychic* well-being (happiness) and therefore, 'does not need to fasten pleasure about his life like a necklace'.[11]

But there is something else hidden in Aristotle's concept. Again, he holds that there is a state for *man*, for *all men*, analogous to overall health. That is, all men at birth possess a shared area of *human potential*, they share a *human nature* that allows them to live roughly the same spectrum of ways of life, including the (eudemonically) perfecting life. And finally, there is an assumption which cannot be derived by analysis from Aristotle's concept, but which is implicit throughout, namely, that some men (at least) can know their fellow men well enough to compare the degrees of happiness afforded by various ways of life.

We now have before us the three propositions upon which my whole approach to the problem of objectivity rests: (1) *There is an optimum road of human development in eudemonic terms*, a way of life that perfects man in terms of human fulfilment or happiness, a way of life that produces a sort of man capable of savouring life to the fullest; (2) *men possess a common human nature in potentia*, that is, all men at birth are capable of being moulded by roughly the same spectrum of ways of life, which spectrum includes the perfecting life; (3) *that properly developed men can have empathy with other men*, sufficient empathy to *know* that the perfecting life *is* more fulfilling than other ways of life. Having stated these three propositions, let me go on to elucidate them in the order listed.

Our first proposition may lead to misunderstanding unless one thing is made clear: it does *not* assume that man has a *tendency* to develop along his optimum road. It assumes that men will find life (eudemonically) better if they live in a certain way, but not that they have some built-in motor which pushes them towards living in that way. As far as I know, there is no conclusive evidence that an imperfecting society (one whose way of life produces men with a limited capacity for fulfilment) meets some sort of resistance in moulding men, while a perfecting society does not. An analogy may prove helpful here. Wood has a *grain*, which means that if a carpenter (representing society) cuts *with* the grain, the wood (representing man at birth) will develop into a better artefact than if he cuts *against* the grain. But the grain is passive: wood has no tendency to follow its optimum road of being worked; rather, the carpenter is the sole active force in working the wood. This analogy can cause trouble if pushed farther than intended (sometimes it makes sense to cut against the grain—and there is the carpenter's purpose to be taken into account). When I say that there is a *grain* in human nature, I *merely* mean to dramatize that man's optimum road of development (in eudemonic terms) is *passive*. Aristotle is quite explicit on this point. He says that human perfection is produced neither by the force of Nature nor against the force of Nature. He contrasts man's character with a stone, which has a natural tendency to fall. And he contrasts man's character with a physical organ like the eyes : man is born with a tendency to see but not with a tendency to become a perfected man.[12]

Perhaps it would be helpful to formulate this notion, that there is a grain in human nature, in the language of a present-day psychologist. Erich Fromm's observations convince him that while society conditions its members to develop along certain lines, men react to that conditioning in terms of 'psychological mechanisms',[13] 'specific properties',[14] 'immutable laws',[15] inherent in human nature. These inherent mechanisms are such that if society allows men to relate to one another through mature love (love based on mutual respect) and creative work, men will achieve health defined as the 'optimum of growth and happiness'; but if society forces men to relate in other ways, e.g. master–slave relationships, they will suffer from loss of spontaneity and anxiety. Thus Fromm concludes that we can make cross-cultural eudemonic judgments, we can compare the ways of life of differing societies in terms of how well they allow for human fulfilment.[16] This conclusion takes Fromm beyond Freud, who reserved judgment on the utility of such comparisons.[17] Indeed, Fromm leads a sizeable band of post-Freudians, including Karen Horney, Theodore Reik, Karl Menninger, etc., all of whom hold that a life oriented towards love and meaningful work maximizes human fulfilment.[18]

As for the detail of the perfecting life, despite variations, these psychologists share a surprisingly large area of agreement. Indeed, my own version of the life that frees man's full potential for fulfilment, what I have called the humanist ideal or the life of humane love and creative work, is derived from their works. At this point, keep in mind the qualification indicated in Chapter 3, namely, that no claim is being advanced, either by myself or by these psychologists, that a *perfectly* humane life suits man best. Men may well need a touch of anti-humane behaviour. And I also want to foreshadow something that will assume importance later on : this way of life, which I judge to be *eudemonically* best for mankind, does not match the way of life I judge *morally* best. True, the eudemonically best way of life is characterized by humane involvement ; it allows for a *measure* of heroism. But my highest moral admiration is reserved for the thorough-going moral hero, Aristotle's man of heroic virtue, who may sacrifice his own capacity for a felicitous life, may even demoralize his whole personality, in order to make a world in which most men can find life felicitous.

The above post-Freudians give the humane life (as qualified) a clear eudemonic nod over its chief challenger within the context of western civilization, the life of the superman. They tend to agree with Plato that the superman's show of strength and self-esteem is a façade, that the man who lusts after thrill to power is one who finds nothing worthwhile within himself and therefore, seeks compensation through exploiting others, through a vain attempt to steal something valuable from his fellows.[19] Fromm goes so far as to say that such a personality, founded on a sense of inadequacy and self-loathing, is divided against itself, that the sadist conceals a masochist ;[20] further, since such a man regards everyone as either an inferior or a superior, he is cheated of any sense of comradeship or genuine love.[21] As the reader will notice, this amounts to a charge that, while the superman may find *vividness* of fulfilment in thrill to power, he lacks *harmony* of soul and *breadth* of fulfilment. Karen Horney lends her support to this assessment[22] and perhaps with good reason : as Menninger points out, it is interesting that Hitler, Mussolini, and Trotsky all exhibited a tendency towards self-punishment, that is, all were abstainers, non-smokers, and vegetarians.[23] Finally, note Nietzsche's conviction that the gratification Plato derived from the Doctrine of Ideas was that of *mastering* the

9

world of sense;[24] perhaps the superman *is* an emotional mono-maniac, one who values thrill to power so much because that is the *only* satisfaction he can find no matter where he turns, whether to philosophy, art, human relations, etc.

However, we must be cautious. Marcuse has called into question the observations of what he calls the 'neo-Freudian revisionists'.[25] To be fair to the superman, we must observe him in a society that favours his way of life, that is, some of his misery may have resulted from the stress of alienation, although the case of the Kwakiutls hardly supports such a thesis. At any rate, I hope it is obvious that our first proposition, that a certain way of life perfects man eudemonically, and our humanist supplement to it, that a life oriented towards humane love and creative work is the perfecting life, both state *empirical hypotheses* which can be verified or falsified. Fuller studies by the behavioural sciences, or man's experience with new ways of living, may show that some non-humane way of life maximizes felicity. Or it may emerge that there is *no such thing* as the perfecting life, that is, some men may be *born* such that their happiness can be maximized only in a society of supermen, while others are *born* such that they will most enjoy a humane society. Perhaps this makes it clear why we Aristotelians refer to human history as the 'human experiment' and to the lives various peoples lead as 'life experiments'. We do not mean that the *men involved* adopt some sort of experimental attitude towards their ways of life; rather, we mean that *we* adopt that sort of attitude—that because of our philosophical perspective, we look upon the record of human history (as illuminated by the sciences of man) as a source of *data*, data which can *test* the crucial propositions of political ethics.

Our second proposition, that men possess a common human nature *in potentia*, can be illustrated by way of an arresting analogy drawn from the anthropologist, Ruth Benedict. All men at birth possess much the same potential in terms of the sounds that can be produced by their vocal chords and oral and nasal cavities. From this immense range of shared potential sounds, each language selects out its own three or four dozen sounds for emphasis, one language selecting from one part of the spectrum, another from a very different part. Similarly, we must imagine that all men at birth possess much the same spectrum of potential emotions and behavioural patterns, an immense spectrum from which each culture selects out a portion for emphasis, for example, Kwakiutl culture selected the narrow emotional arc ranging from triumph to shame while Zuni culture places its emphasis on temperance, moderation, and sobriety.[26]

Like all analogies this one must not be taken literally. It is not utilized to suggest that men are born with a variety of traits and that societies make a selection from these as shoppers might select from articles on display. Its purpose is to pose an important question : as we study society after society, we find that different peoples live in very different ways, we discover an immense range of values and behaviour ; how are we to interpret these data? Are these ways of life *alternatives* for all mankind at least at birth, each man having hidden in him the *potential* to adapt to a variety of ways of life, to develop the interests, attitudes, and relationships they entail? Or does the fact that all men are found to be leading *only one* of these lives and *not the others* show that each man's genetic endowment has an affinity for a certain way of life and stands as a barrier to adaptation to another? Those who take the latter position attempt to explain such affinity and resistance by positing the *genetic determination* of personality types : certain men are born to become supermen and cannot become humane men even in the appropriate cultural setting; the difference between Kwakiutls and Zunis must be correlated with differences in their genetic structures.

Benedict emphatically rejects the biological interpretation of personal and behavioural traits. She notes both that very different racial types can be accommodated by one culture, e.g. a Chinese or Negro child raised in Paris becomes a true Parisian Frenchman, and that groups which are closely related develop very different cultures, e.g. the Shoshonean Indian subgroup includes Apollonian as well as Dionysian tribes. She concludes that genetic flexibility plus cultural differences account for the tremendous variation in temperament we find throughout mankind, not genetic rigidity plus genetic differences.[27] On the other side of the ledger, some of the 'twin studies', studies of identical twins raised in different environments, have been cited as evidence that personality *is* genetically determined.[28] The novelist William March has even developed the notion that a child can be born to be a sadist or murderer.[29] However, recent evaluations of the twin studies tend to conclude that personality, as distinct from physique or intelligence, is more a product of environment than heredity.

Certain common-sense qualifications are in order, of course. Einstein was born with a greater capacity for mathematics and Mozart with a greater talent for composing music than most of us, to say the least; no doubt, these hereditary differences affected their capacity for happiness, e.g. I am unable to appreciate a piece of music non-discursively as Mozart claims he could. Our second proposition does not assume that all men have identical heredity or that heredity is a null factor; it merely assumes that all men are born capable of being acculturated by a variety of human societies, by Zuni society, Kwakiutl society, a Nietzschean society, a humane society, etc. Their heredity will make a difference in the *variant* of their society's way of life that they live: it is one thing to be a humane carpenter and another to be a humane genius; it is one thing to be an intelligent 'superman' and another to be an unimaginative one. In sum, we assume only that some variant of the perfecting life and its competitors is open to all men and that whatever way of life men follow will have an important influence on their happiness.

Our third proposition asserts that (eudemonically) perfected men can *empathize* with other men sufficiently to *know* that their own way of life is more felicitous than its competitors. Discussions about empathy always seem to arouse scepticism, but certainly we all possess the ability to experience or assess the emotions of others to some degree. We meet a friend and, before any words have passed, we somehow know that something has happened to demoralize him since we last saw him, we just *feel* an atmosphere of malaise. As Katz has pointed out, every one of the sciences of man assumes empathy in some form: biology speaks of 'instinctive reverberation', psychoanalysis of 'identification', social psychology of 'role-taking', and sociology of 'mutual understanding' within the in-group.[30] As for anthropology, Redfield and Kluckholm have stressed the necessity of empathizing with the members of the culture under study.[31] It is significant that Benedict, often hailed as the apostle of cultural relativity, continually assumes that she can empathize sufficiently to make cross-cultural eudemonic judgments. She tells us that Dobuans live out 'man's worst nightmares', that Kwakiutl culture afforded 'a zest which it is difficult to match among other peoples', that the Zunis are a 'mildly happy populace'.[32]

All of us possess a considerable ability to empathize as infants. Before we are capable of verbal communication, we must be able to empathize, particularly with our parents, if we are to survive and develop. As for the ability of perfected men to empathize with others, it appears that humane men often retain more of the child's capacity for this than do other personality types, e.g. authoritarians, sado-masochists, etc.[33] But again, we must eschew unwarranted confidence. We may well discover a people so alien that we cannot achieve sufficient empathy to form even a rough and probable estimate of the fulfilments afforded by their way of life.

Finally, I wish to add something to what has become a persistent theme, the theme that all three of our propositions are empirical hypotheses which can be verified or falsified. It is often thought that Aristotle's ethics was undermined by the collapse of metaphysics. But Aristotle's ethics actually rests upon his *psychology*, which in turn rests upon his metaphysics. If modern social science can provide a new foundation for his psychology, his assumptions about man, then we can salvage his ethics. Another view often expressed is that evolution undermines Aristotle's ethics by demonstrating the mutability of species.[34] Recall that it was Darwin who eroded belief in ethical truth in nineteenth-century America. To be frank, I must say I find widespread acceptance of this view difficult to comprehend. If evolution had produced two 'ethical species' of men, two types of men whose human potential did not significantly overlap, Aristotle would simply have granted that what was the perfecting life for one was *not* the perfecting life for the other; indeed, Aristotle thought (erroneously) that there *were* two ethical species of men, that is, he thought some men were born natural slaves. And if evolution in the future so alters human nature that our three propositions do not hold, we Aristotelians will of course abandon our views on the perfecting life. Why should the life that (eudemonically) perfects man also perfect this new creature which is postman? Certainly if someone told Aristotle that man was to be exterminated and replaced by Martians, Aristotle would have said that we would have to study *their* nature to see what way of life, if any, would perfect *them*.

*   *   *

I now wish to put forward the following contention: that (granted our analysis of happiness) our three propositions about human nature are *collectively equivalent* to asserting that a certain way of life has objective or non-partisan eudemonic value. At this point, the clarity and correctness of my concept of objective status assume supreme importance; therefore, I would like to refine and defend my concept. The best way of doing this is to go back to our old dispute between a humane man and a Nietzschean. However, I want to alter the dispute in two ways: first, since I am attempting to show that a certain way of life has non-partisan status in terms of *eudemonic* goodness, I wish to make it a dispute about the *eudemonic* value of their respective ways of life; and second, I want to make them carry their dispute a bit further, to take a look at what they might say to one another in such a dispute.

Imagine, then, a humane man and a Nietzschean arguing about the eudemonic value of their differing ways of life. And recall that these men *really do* have conflicting fundamental values, that they *really are* a humane man and a Nietzschean: one finds felicity in a life characterized by humane love and creative work, while the other finds felicity in the superman's life, a life oriented towards thrill to power.

In such a dispute, the humane man might try to argue that his way of life afforded him greater happiness than his opponent enjoyed by way of a superman's life. He might concede that thrill to power was as *vivid* a fulfilment as humane fulfilments, e.g. those of comradeship and love; but he would go on to claim that the superman, in being limited to thrill to power, lacked *breadth* of fulfilment and that the superman, since his sense of triumph was often followed by a sense of worthlessness, an enervating opposite, lacked a *harmonious* emotional life. However, at this point, the Nietzschean might well answer back: 'Even if I grant that your way of life affords you more felicity than mine affords me, so what? The only experiences I actually have, the only fulfilments I actually enjoy, are *my own*. I do not experience the felicity your life gives you, any more than I do your coughs, cuts, or laughter. So let us say that while your way of life is eudemonically good for you, it is not for me. And whatever empathy you may have with me, certainly I know the fulfilments my life affords me more intimately than you do. Just as you are the best judge of the eudemonic value of your way of life, I am the best judge of mine.'

We seem to be at a loss, a symptom perhaps of the fact that we have not sufficiently clarified our notion of objectivity. Let us try to help ourselves by analysing an interesting dispute in the realm of facts. Imagine a man with 20/20 vision and a man suffering from astigmatism disputing about something, let us say whether or not there is a tree twenty yards from where they stand. Presumably, the man with 20/20 vision would assert, with some impatience, that he saw a tree very clearly and that his opponent could see nothing but a blur, as they both very well knew. His opponent might reply: 'Granted that your vision is clearer than mine, still I actually have only *my own* visual experiences, not yours. You see a tree but I do not, so let us say that it is there for you but not for me. You can rely on your vision to establish the facts of your world, but I will rely on my vision to verify facts in my world.' But here, of course, the man with 20/20 vision would not be at a loss at all. He would tell the man with astigmatism to walk ten paces forward and then say: 'You could not predict what you would see when you did that, but I could—I knew you would see a tree. Therefore, my visual experiences were not merely better verifiers of fact for me; my visual experiences gave *me* better knowledge of the facts of *your* world than your experiences gave *you* !'*

If I am not mistaken, we have hit on a way to elucidate our concept of objective status. The tree had objective factual status because it existed for those who did not appreciate its existence as well as for the man who did. The visual experiences of the man with 20/20 vision were veridical, had objective status, because they were worthy of note by those who did not possess them as well as by the man who did. And note that their status corresponds to the definition of objectivity we have assumed all along, that is: a thing has objective status when men should recognize its status whether they actually do so or not. Note also, in the above example, that the status of the tree and the status of the visual experiences of the man with 20/20 vision are obviously interrelated: it was only because these two men

---

* I am well aware that in making our man with astigmatism talk about trees existing for some people and not for others, I have made him use the word 'exist' in an absurd way. However, I must do this if we are to imagine someone contending that physical objects have only non-objective existence. His words seem absurd because we know very well that we all live in the same physical world (where trees exist for everybody) and thus, use the word 'exist' only in an objective sense. But again, if I am to show *why* using it in a non-objective sense *is* absurd, I must put that usage into someone's mouth.

lived in a *shared physical universe* (where the same objects existed for both) that the man with sound vision could assert that *his own* visual experiences were better *for his opponent* than *his opponent's* were.

Now let us go back to our Nietzschean and see what we can say to him, perhaps something like this : 'It is true that you know your own fulfilments more intimately than we do. But still, when you concede that our way of life affords us more happiness than you find in your life, you have conceded something quite significant. For when a man assesses the (eudemonic) *value* of his way of life, he must take into account not only the fulfilments he has *gained* thereby but also the fulfilments he has *lost* thereby. For example, if you were assessing the value of your education at Oxford, you would have to take into account the educational experience you missed by not going to the University of Otago. Since the latter would have been more enlightening, Oxford not only opened certain intellectual doors for you ; it also shut distinctly more important doors—assuming, of course, that you were eligible for both universities. Similarly, your way of life has not only *opened the door* to certain fulfil-ments ; it has also *shut the door* to the greater felicity you would have obtained had you lived a humane life—assum-ing, of course, that you were capable of such a life. You admit that we know the felicity you have lost, the felicity of the humane life, better than you. Since it is greater than the felicity you have gained, and since *both are relevant* to assessing the eudemonic value of your way of life, we can make this claim : our felicitous experience gives *us* know-ledge of something more important in assessing the value of *your* life than your experience gives *you*.'

In sum, this dispute with the Nietzschean has led us to claim objective eudemonic value on behalf of our way of life. Just as the tree was there for the man with astigmatism whether he saw it or not, so *our* way of life is eudemonically best *for our opponent* whether *he* values it or not—assuming again, that he can live our life and attain its greater felicity. Just as a man's 20/20 vision gave him better knowledge of the facts of the astigmatic's world than the latter's vision afforded him, so *our* fulfilling experience gives us better knowledge of the value of the *superman's* way of life than *his* fulfilling experience gives him. And note another parallel: it was the fact that the man with 20/20 vision and the astigmatic lived in a *shared physical universe in actuality* that paved the way for objectivity, for it meant that the former's vision was superior in exploring a world which was *his opponent's* as well as his own; and now, it is the fact that we and the superman possess a *shared human nature in potentia* that paves the way for objectivity, for it means that our way of life has better exploited the potentialities of a nature which is *our opponent's* as well as our own.

We can now appreciate the importance of our second proposition, that men at birth are capable of living roughly the same spectrum of lives. After all, if supermen were born as members of a separate ethical species, born to be supermen with our way of life foreclosed, we could hardly indict a superman's way of life with having cheated him of the greater fulfilments of our own. You may ask why it is so important whether or not his *genetic make-up* forecloses the humane life, when millions are born into societies where *social conditions* foreclose it as a realistic alternative. But that the ways of life of these societies foreclose the (eudemonically) perfecting life is precisely what allows us to indict *their ways of life*; if genetic factors meant that the door to the perfecting life was *never open*, we could hardly indict their ways of life for *having closed it*! Environmentalism, often thought antagonistic to a classical approach to ethics, is, to this degree at least, a friend.

*   *   *

Given the use to which they have been put, I can hardly hope that my three propositions about human nature will escape criticism. As I see it, my case for objective status in the realm of eudemonic goodness raises three problems, problems which have to do with the nature of happiness, the flexibility of men, and the need for empathy respectively.

Our first problem can be best posed by being put in the mouth of a critic: 'Rather than emphasizing the privacy of his fulfilling experiences, your Nietzschean would have done better to emphasize the partisan nature of your concept of happiness. Whenever you compare the humane life with that of the superman, and whenever you assess the comparative felicity of Zunis, Kwakiutls, etc., you assume that men share a certain notion of happiness, or at least that a certain notion has some sort of cross-personal validity. Actually, what each man *means* by happiness is linked to *what makes him happy*: some men define happiness in terms of competition and money and power; others define it in terms of co-operation and creativity. Indeed, our very notion of happiness is determined by our peculiar goals and interests, by the peculiar activities and fulfilling experiences each of us enjoys. For example, a Nietzschean's concept of happiness is likely to emphasize vividness because his way of life features thrill to power, an unusually vivid fulfilment; while a humane man's concept will emphasize harmony of soul as well as vividness, essentially because co-operative human relationships are productive of a harmonious emotional world. Even if two notions of happiness both emphasize vividness, this does not necessarily indicate common ground in that the concepts of vividness may be linked to two different kinds of fulfilling experience which are not comparable. For example, the vividness of thrill to power is not really comparable to the vivid emotions which usually attend love relationships.

'In other words, thanks to their different notions of happiness, men can disagree just as much about happiness as they do about moral goodness; and no one has a right to claim that his notion or the eudemonic assessments based on it are worthy of regard from those who hold a different notion. Which means that your Nietzschean has every right to dismiss comparative assessments based on your concept of happiness. Which in turn means that he has a right to discount the "evidence" of the post-Freudians you cite. This is not to say that these latter give a false account of the psychological effects certain ways of life have on various men; perhaps men do develop broad and vivid fulfilling experiences in a harmonious emotional world by way of a life oriented towards humane love and creative work. Rather, it is a matter of their assessing the psychological effects of various ways of life in terms of a partisan notion of happiness, in terms that count a man fully happy only if he enjoys a broad, vivid, and harmonious world of fulfilling experience.'

By way of rebuttal, I will analyse the two major points made by the above critic: that our notions of happiness are tied to the specific interests, or activities, or fulfilments which make us happy (and therefore, are inevitably partisan notions); and that my Nietzschean and I merely hold two differing notions of happiness, neither of which has cross-personal validity (which is to say, I have no right to claim that my way of life is best *for him*—it is eudemonically best merely in terms of *my* notion of happiness).

The difficulty with the thesis that our notions of happiness are tied to what makes us happy is this: it cannot account for something of great importance, the man who radically alters the specific things which make him happy and yet, says that he has achieved greater happiness. I do not, of course, refer to someone who has increased his happiness merely by getting more of what he always wanted, e.g. a miser who inherits a fortune. I refer to the sort of man who was once engrossed in a competitive struggle for wealth and prestige and found a certain satisfaction therein, but who then changed his way of life, embraced new interests, new ideas of what is important, new relationships, and even began to experience new emotions and fulfilments. After all, there are many such: in recent years, thousands of young Americans have abandoned competitive ideals and careers in favour of attempts to build human relationships founded on affection and sympathy and attempts to develop their creativity. Now, when such a man tells us that he is happier than he used to be, how can we make sense of what he is saying *if* concepts of happiness are tied to the specific things which make men happy? Again, he has *radically altered* what makes him happy, he has *replaced* one set of things with another. Are we to say to him : 'Happiness must be defined in terms of specifics. You used to define it in terms of competition and money and a sense of victory or success; now you must do so in terms of the fulfilments which attend humane love and creative work. Therefore, you cannot make the sort of comparison you want to—you cannot say you are *happier* than you used to be, but only that happiness means *something different* to you now than it used to.'

In effect, by linking the notion of happiness to specific things which make men happy, we leave the man who has replaced one set of things by another with *no basis* for eudemonic comparisons—with nothing to say except that he has replaced one notion of happiness by another. To give another example, imagine someone who abandons the usual competitive scramble to become not just a humane man, but a humane mystic, who adds to his sense of union with others the creative task of achieving the mystical consciousness of union with all. If he tells us he is a happier man because the sense of beatitude (which attends his mystical consciousness) is *more vivid* than his original fulfilments, those of prestige and success, are we to tell him : 'You cannot say that; vividness is linked to specific fulfilments and therefore, the vividness of your new fulfilments is not comparable to the vividness of those you have abandoned'?

In order to account for such assessments, assessments in which men make a eudemonic comparison between a new set of fulfilments and an old set, I believe we must posit a notion of happiness *detached* from specific activities, or interests, or fulfilments. Indeed, when asked what they mean, the men in question do not talk in terms of specifics, they do not merely list what they once enjoyed (money, prestige, winning, etc.) and then list what they now enjoy (relaxed and non-competitive and empathetic human relationships, creative work, etc.). To do this would be useless because it introduces *no comparative dimension*. Rather, they tend to talk in terms of categories detached from such things, to say that they feel more alive (vividness) or have escaped anxiety (harmony) or have discovered a whole new world of fulfilments in their relationships with others (breadth). This does not prove that men must talk in terms of *all three* of these categories when making such comparisons; it may be that Nietzscheans and Kwakiutls would tend to use only vividness, that Zunis would tend to use only harmony, etc. I will postpone this question, the question of the cross-personal relevance of my three categories, for a moment. At present, I am arguing only that we must posit 'detached' categories of *some sort*.

However, I want to give my critic his due. Sometimes we merely wish to make explicit what makes us happy at a particular time, e.g. 'happiness is a good five cent cigar', and then we *do* use the word 'happiness' to refer to specific activities and the fulfilments to which they give rise. It is primarily when a man compares himself as he is with himself as he was (or one man with another, or one society with another) that he needs eudemonic terms detached from specifics. I am tempted to call the specific things which make us happy the *content* of happiness and to say that the detached terms we use to make certain comparisons refer to the *form* of happiness. For note that terms like vividness and harmony and breadth are *not* detached in an absolute sense: they refer to something, namely to certain characteristics of our emotional world, whether it features lively fulfilments, a harmonious 'tone', etc.; they are formal or detached *only* in the sense of refering to something other than the content of specific fulfilments. Recall our humane mystic above. When he compares his sense of beatitude with the fulfilments he has left behind (basking in the sunshine of success and the envy of his neighbours) in terms of vividness, he is clearly using vividness as a term detached from the content of any particular fulfilment.

Talking about the content and form of happiness is quite likely to put many readers off—everyone does not have the same taste for Aristotelian terminology that the author does. As always, I am quite willing to be flexible about phrasing just so long as the substance of my point is left intact. I am even willing to say that when a man radically alters what makes him happy, he has traded one concept of happiness for another; after all, such a man often says 'I never knew what happiness was before', which seems to imply that he has discovered a new concept of happiness in some sense. However, I am not willing to leave it at that. If the phrase 'concept of happiness' is to be tied to specifics, there will have to be a new phrase which is not, perhaps '*overriding* concept of happiness'. For I must insist on some sort of notion of happiness which allows a man who has radically altered his way of life, his interests, and relation-ships, and fulfilments, to compare his new kind of happiness with his old. And again, such a notion must be detached from, or override, or transcend the specific things which make him happy, both the old set of specifics and the new. In other words, if something like my broad, vivid, and harmonious concept of happiness did not exist, it would have to be invented.

This brings us to our critic's other point, his contention that my concept of happiness lacks cross-personal validity. For his reaction to my argument thus far would almost certainly be as follows: 'Granted that we must posit a concept of happiness with detached categories of some sort, why should your Nietzschean not pick and choose from among your three categories? Why should he not say that his concept of happiness includes *only vividness* (in terms of which his way of life gets high marks) and omits harmony (in terms of which he comes off badly)? Until you deal with this question, he can contend that you hold *one* formal or overriding notion of happiness and that he holds *another*— and that neither notion is valid for the man who rejects it.'

In my view, our critic has not discovered a way out for Nietzscheans. Indeed, *if* a Nietzschean were to take a stand along the above lines, I would have an answer ready: 'Of course you experience periodic vivid fulfilments, but what goes on the rest of the time?—certainly your emotional life continues to flow in between its high points just like anyone else's. You can hardly say that these "in between times" are irrelevant to your happiness in that a superman would be less happy if his victories were less frequent and the intervals between them became longer and longer, which is understandable, given that they tend to be filled by periods of anxiety and tension. Now if these intervals (which make up much the greater portion of our emotional life) were filled with something positive, with a sense of well-being and spontaneity, and if this came about *without any sacrifice* in either the frequency or vividness of your periodic fulfilments (*which is crucial*—see below), do you really believe your happiness would not be increased? Since you have not enjoyed much harmony of soul, there may be a problem of imagination here, so let me put it this way: imagine that your sense of anxiety and tension grew more intense, so that between thrills to power you felt so demoralized as to be virtually suicidal; under those circumstances, I doubt that you would still argue that a certain level of emotional harmony was irrelevant to your happiness. After all, when you go from demoralization to a tolerable level of tension, you do not say to yourself: "Now *is* harmony of soul relevant to my notion of happiness?"—rather, you *experience* the change as a eudemonic improvement. And if finding life tolerable during these intervals is relevant, what about finding them more than tolerable, finding them filled with something much more positive?'

Actually, I doubt that our Nietzschean would argue as above, would argue that a certain level of vividness *with* heightened harmony was no more felicitous than that same level of vividness *without*. I believe he would eschew such an argument for another, one which bears a superficial resemblance to the above but is in fact quite different. That is, he might claim that increased harmony is bought at the price of decreased vividness, e.g. he might say: 'To become humane may mean a gain in harmony of soul, but one must give up or at least mute the most vivid fulfilment of all, thrill to power.' This is a much more plausible position, for it does *not* discount harmony as irrelevant to happiness; rather it takes harmony into account and merely argues that the factors which make up happiness are *functionally interrelated*, that a certain way of life may increase one at the expense of another. However, while this last is true as a general observation, there seems to be no reason to grant the truth of the specific claim which our Nietzschean has put forward. For one thing, humane men can enjoy a sense of mastery closely akin to thrill to power, e.g. mastery over the forces of nature. For another, the behaviour of men suggests that thrill to power, however vivid, is no more vivid than those fulfilments open to humane men, the fulfilments of love, comradeship, creativity in the arts, solving a problem, beatitude, etc. Indeed, there is indirect evidence that the Nietzscheans themselves suspect that this is the case. They are quick to claim that the fulfilments we have listed are mere 'variations' on thrill to power, which is revealing in that one does not bother to define rivals out of existence (much less incorporate them) unless one suspects that they are potent.

We have neglected the category of breadth of fulfilment up to this point, primarily because it is less important than the other two. However, I do not want this remark misunderstood in that I stand by my claim that it is a component of happiness. If a man can add a new sort of fulfilment to those he has already with no sacrifice in vividness (without spreading his capacity for feeling too thin) and with no sacrifice in harmony, he is certainly the happier for it. Further, if breadth diminishes to the vanishing point, a man enjoys no vivid fulfilments at all. I merely mean to say that breadth is interrelated with the other factors which make up happiness and that all peoples, as far as I know, sacrifice maximizing it if they can gain heightened vividness or harmony thereby. And it seems significant that no one ever suggests that happiness involves *only breadth*, while such suggestions are made concerning vividness and harmony. Just by way of clarification, when speaking of breadth, I refer to breadth of fulfilment, not activity. When we limit our activities to a few areas, rather than doing many things badly, we may actually achieve a wider range of fulfilment, may replace areas which give us no real satisfaction with one or two which afford us a rich variety of satisfactions.

Before leaving our first problem, a problem engendered by my first proposition about human nature, I want to say one more thing: my solution must not be allowed to obscure the fact that my first proposition (that a certain way of life is the eudemonically perfecting life) can be expressed in a variety of ways. To be explicit, it can be expressed in language which links notions of happiness to ways of life, *if* we take care to avoid the verbal trap such language sets. And to be specific, as men turn from other ways of living towards humanism, I *welcome* saying that they exchange old concepts of happiness for a new one—just so long as we add that men *really are happier* for entering a world of broad and vivid fulfilling experiences set against a harmonious emotional background. It detracts not one whit from the stature of the perfecting life to say that it teaches men a new concept of happiness in terms of which they find life more felicitous—that it offers mankind a concept which expands the horizons of human fulfilment.

*   *   *

Unfortunately, having defended my case that a certain way of life, one skewed towards humane love and creative work, has objective eudemonic value, I must now add an unpalatable qualification. For our second problem, which grows out of my second proposition about human nature, is much more troublesome than our first. The problem is not that the proposition in question is false, but that it fails to take certain facts into account, namely: while men at birth may be capable of roughly the same spectrum of ways of life, they lose flexibility as age and acculturation solidify their personalities.

For example, a Nietzschean at forty might well find it

traumatic to alter his way of life radically; such an attempt might lead, not to greater felicity, but to the disintegration of his whole personality. It may just be too late for him to develop new interests, forge new relationships, experience new emotions. If his priorities are fixed so that he is incapable of interest in anything but triumph and domination, he will find that new activities add no zest to his life—that he cannot replace thrill to power with something equally vivid. If he has lost his capacity to learn to love and empathize with others, he can hardly hope to enter the emotional world which encourages and attends relationships based on mutual regard. In sum, an attempt to live the humane life would not *develop him as a person*, but would become the mechanical acting out of a part, the sort of charade which opens up a demoralizing gap between feeling and behaviour. And this is not a problem confined to individuals. Something similar seems to be true of certain 'primitive' cultures; it appears that certain tribes have developed cultures which are so rigid and inflexible that any attempt on their part to incorporate new values (e.g. humane ones) might bring on collective demoralization. Now if we are dealing with someone whose personal history or cultural environment has produced this sort of rigidity, let us say a Nietzschean at forty, we can hardly recommend the humane life to him as a viable alternative. True, we can reiterate our indictment of his way of life, we can point out that his way of life has not only shut the door to maximum felicity but also shut it *permanently*. But this does not alter the fact that the humane life is no longer (eudemonically) better for him than the superman's life, that given what he now is, he might well maximize his felicity by continuing with the superman's life.

The above, that men do not continue to possess a shared human nature *even in potentia* throughout their lives, seems to me to qualify seriously the objective validity of the perfecting life. Unlike the tree which was there for *all men* whether they knew it or not, the perfecting life is (eudemonically) best *only* for men who are not rigid partisans of some alternative way of life, who are not inflexibly committed to some other alternative. I believe that this sheds some light on the significance of traditional Christian beliefs for the problem of objectivity in ethics. Until recently, most Christians held: that however set a man might be in his sinful ways, if he turned to God, God's grace would help him to alter his way of life successfully; and that even if such a man were on his death bed, he had an eternity in heaven to discover the greater felicity that his new way of life would entail. These beliefs amount to an assertion that men *never lose* their shared human nature *in potentia*, their capacity to live the perfecting life, and therefore salvage the case for objective eudemonic value. Given such a perspective, there never comes a time, this side of hell, when the perfecting life is not worthy of regard from *all men*, including *all* of those who do not value it.

Once we abandon the claim that the perfecting life has *objective* eudemonic value, what sort of status can we claim for it? I would say that it posseses *non-partisan* eudemonic value. We can no longer say that the perfecting life is better for *all men* than whatever ways of life they happen to value, that is, its advantage over competing ways of life is not strictly analogous to the distinction between objective and subjective status in the realm of fact. But we can still say that it is better for *all men who are not partisans*, who are not inflexibly committed to a certain way of life, than whatever life they may value. Its advantage over competing ways of life, let us say the superman's, is this: the superman can claim only that his way of life has partisan eudemonic value, that it is best only for its partisans; while we can claim not only that the humane life is best for its partisans, but that it has non-partisan validity as well, that it is (eudemonically) best for uncommitted mankind. Unless I am mistaken, this distinction between non-partisan and partisan validity is similar to the ancients' distinction between the *natural* and the *conventional*, between a way of life of only conventional value and the perfecting life, which not only suited those living it but also was in accord with human nature! And this sort of 'natural' or non-partisan status, while not equivalent to objective status, is nearer to it than to a realm where non-objectivity holds sway, e.g. a realm like the hedonic value of soft drinks. For we can still say to non-partisan mankind that *our* way of life is better for *them* than *their* way of life is.

At this point, the reader may well want to pose an objection, namely, whether or not there is any portion of mankind that can be described as non-partisan. When the champions of various ways of life appeal to mankind, they are not speaking into an evaluative vacuum; they are addressing men *all of whom* are 'biased', not in the pejorative meaning of the word of course but in that all of us have our own values and inclinations, possess values which render us more partial to some ways of life than others. If the perfecting life is more valid only for non-partisan mankind is it more valid for anyone?

This objection ignores the distinction between men who are partisan in the sense of being *inflexibly committed* to a certain way of life and those who are 'partisan' *merely* in the sense of being biased, those who value a certain way of life but are still flexible enough to change. The perfecting life lacks eudemonic validity only for men who are inflexibly committed to another way of life, only for men for whom it is no longer a viable option like our Nietzschean at forty. It has validity for those inflexibly committed to it, those whose values bias them in its favour, and those biased against it but still capable of adapting to it. An ideological appeal on its behalf to these latter may, because of their antagonism, be ineffective; but such an appeal is still *valid* as far as they are concerned, that is, its claim that the perfecting life is (eudemonically) better for them still has non-rhetorical significance. And if someone goes further to object that all men are not only biased but also inflexibly committed, that all men are so committed that no one is really free to make a significant choice between two ways of life, I can only say that this deserves serious consideration but that I will not deal with it here. For such an objection, if defensible, renders all debate about how we should live trivial; it does not threaten my neo-Aristotelian approach in any special way, but urges us to say 'alas, all ideology' and indeed, 'alas, all ethics'.

Just to avoid any possible misunderstanding, I will use the terms *partisan* and *committed* to refer only to those inflexibly committed to a certain way of life; and I will use the terms *non-partisan* and *uncommitted* to refer to all other men, including those biased in favour of a certain way of life but not inflexibly committed to it. Now if I am granted that a significant portion of mankind are not partisans (in my sense), note that my concession that we must abandon objective validity on behalf of the perfecting life in favour of non-partisan validity is not very serious *in the context of ideological competition*. In political terms, whether or not my way of life is valid for a Nietzschean at forty, whether or not it is valid for a man who can never adopt it, is rather academic. When ideologues, the partisans of various ways of life, compete for the allegiance of mankind, they do not appeal to those who cannot change; they aim at the uncommitted, the non-partisan portion of mankind, and if an ideologue has an advantage over his competitors here, he has the advantage that counts. A Trotskyite, opposed by a Communist, wants to believe his way of life is better for the masses; he does not worry about an élite inflexibly committed to capitalism.

Of course, most of us do not have the same illusions about the mass of men, even in complex highly industrialized societies, that Trotskyites have about the proletariat. Still, there seems to be no reason for too much gloom in the ranks of humanist ideologues. There are many signs that the youth of these societies are in a state of ferment, that they are flexible enough so that they are *capable* of a turn towards humanism. Whether they *actually are* turning in that direction, or whether they *will* do so, is another matter, one which might well inspire a certain degree of pessimism.

Our third problem stems from a failure to clarify *the role* of my third proposition about human nature, a proposition which states that properly developed men (humane men) must be able to develop sufficient empathy with others to *know* that their way of life is more fulfilling than other lives. Now, as the reader may have noticed, this proposition did not play a very significant part when I stated my case in favour of the objective (later altered to non-partisan) eudemonic value of the humane life (see pp. 124–8). Further, my references to empathy since then emphasize its contribution to living a humane life, emphasize the difficulty of attempting to live in accord with humane ideals unless one can develop empathy with one's fellow men. In other words, ambiguity about the role of empathy seems to leave me with the following dilemma: either it is not necessary for my case and therefore, my third proposition is superfluous; or it is necessary for my case and therefore, biases it—by resting it on something (developing empathy) which humane men value more than their opponents do.

This dilemma dissolves if we clearly distinguish the *epistemological* role of empathy from its role as a *valued character trait*. To spell out the former, my third proposition is not a pre-requisite for the existence of the perfecting life. Even if it were false, even if no one (not just humane men) had sufficient empathy with others to compare levels of happiness, there could still be a way of life with non-partisan eudemonic value, a life which opened the door to maximum felicity while other ways of life shut that door. However, under those conditions, no one could *know* that the perfecting life *was* eudemonically best. There is, of course, nothing logically impossible about such a situation: something can be true and yet, men may lack the faculties to know that it is true. As for the other role of empathy, it is undeniable that it is a faculty or trait which humane men in particular value. But this does nothing to bias its epistemological role. The humanist ideal also includes a healthy body with healthy sense organs. Yet, without functional eyes, we would have difficulty knowing many of the truths of astronomy. The fact that humanists value a knowledge-giver does not make it any less necessary for gaining knowledge. Empathy would remain a prerequisite to knowing the perfecting life as such even if it were valued only by supermen.

I do not want to over-emphasize the epistemological role of empathy. In many cases, we do not need much of it to tell when men suffer from anxiety, lack of spontaneity, etc.; they exhibit symptoms which are clear enough. However, if the perfecting life is to be known, there must be some proposition which is true and which states that at least some men have the ability to compare levels of fulfilment. Since all that is required is that *some men* have this ability, it may seem gratuitous to single out perfected or humane men as those who need sufficient empathy. This last *is* unnecessary in one sense: for epistemological purposes, it would make no difference if only supermen had the ability to know that a certain way of life (not theirs) was the perfecting life. But in the context of our dispute, our dispute with the Nietz-schean, it would be terribly embarrassing to be dependent on *him* to know that we were right and he was wrong!

*   *   *

Have we really, at long last, resolved our dispute with the Nietzschean? Such disputes, disputes which reflect divergent fundamental values, are supposed to be unresolvable. The argument runs as follows: if the two disputants have no shared ground on values, their only shared ground will be concerning facts; thus, if values cannot be logically derived from facts, the dispute must be unresolvable.

It may be remembered that I promised to deal with this argument, which attempts to show that any case for objectivity in ethics must be *logically incoherent*, early in this work (see p. 51). In a word, my opinion of it is this: it is unbeatable on its face, but it is just *not applicable* to the sort of dispute we are primarily concerned with, that is, an ideological dispute as distinct from a dispute about personal ethics. Let me clarify this point by focusing on our humane man and our Nietzschean and attempting to state the precise sense in which their dispute is resolvable: (1) In so far as the humane man and the Nietzschean have nothing in common about the way of life they value, and in so far as the Nietzschean's inflexibility means that they never can have such values in common, the dispute cannot be resolved *as a personal dispute*, a dispute as to how the Nietzschean should live; (2) but in so far as the Nietzschean can be brought to a shared opinion about values, about what way of life non-partisan mankind would find best, the dispute can be resolved *as an ideological dispute*, a dispute about whose way of life possesses non-partisan validity. And to bring him around, we would try to present *evidence*, the evidence of mankind's experiment with differing ways of life and their fulfilments—though again, note that this would render the dispute resolvable only in terms of eudemonic, as distinct from moral, goodness.

I should add that if our Nietzschean merely has a bias in favour of the superman's life and is *not* an inflexible partisan, then *he himself* is a member of non-partisan mankind, that is, he is not only our opponent but also a member of our 'ideological audience'. Under these circumstances, we may be able to resolve our dispute with him on a personal level; we can try to find evidence that it is not too late for him to become humane and discover a heightened felicity. Reverting to viewing him solely as an opponent in an ideological dispute, I hope that certain phrases, such as those which describe ourselves and a Nietzschean debating about what life is best for 'non-partisan mankind', do not convince the reader that I am distorting his position or loading the dice against him. Let me again make clear that I do not apply such phrases to a Nietzschean in a literal sense; they are not intended to obscure the fact that he would say that the superman's life is suitable not for mankind but only for an élite subspecies of mankind, an élite whose genetic endowment renders them capable of becoming supermen. And let me also make clear that I am quite willing to argue with him on his own ground: if he thinks that he can supply a genetic criterion which allows us to distinguish a class of potential supermen at birth, I will be happy to study *their* varying life experiments to see which way of life does the most to perfect *them* eudemonically.

It is quite possible, of course, that even if the evidence of the human experiment damns his cause, our Nietzschean will not actually give in; perhaps because this evidence is not available to him (as an authoritarian personality, he might lack the empathy with others needed to realize that a way of life other than his own maximizes felicity) or because he chooses to ignore it. But this would merely mean that our ideological dispute is unresolvable *in practice*. It is still resolvable *in theory* in that we can convict him of one of these sins: being blind to or ignoring evidence; an error of logic; misusing words.

NOTES

[1] Georg Henrik von Wright, *The Varieties of Goodness* (London: Routledge & Kegan Paul, 1963), p. 121.

[2] *Ibid.*, p. 11.

[3] *Ibid.*, p. 98.

[4] *Ibid.*, p. 119.

[5] Ruth Benedict, *Patterns of Culture* (Boston & New York: Houghton Mifflin, 1934).

[6] G. E. Moore, *Principia Ethica* (Cambridge: The University Press, 1903), p. 17.

[7] Plato, *Republic*, iv. 435–43.

[8] Plato, *Phaedrus*, 246–7, 253–6.

[9] Plato, *Republic*, iv. 444.

[10] Aristotle, *Nicomachean Ethics*, iii. 4. 1113^a. 25–35.

[11] *Ibid.*, i. 8. 1099^a. 15–16.

[12] *Ibid.*, ii. 1. 1103^a. 18–35.

[13] Erich Fromm, *Escape from Freedom* (New York: Holt, Rinehart & Winston, 1941), pp. 14–15.

[14] Erich Fromm, *Man for Himself* (New York: Rinehart, 1947), pp. 21–4.

[15] Erich Fromm, *Psychoanalysis and Religion* (New Haven: Yale University Press, 1959), p. 74.

[16] Fromm, *Escape from Freedom*, pp. 138–41.

[17] Sigmund Freud, *Civilization and Its Discontents* (London: Hogarth Press, 1930), pp. 141–2.

[18] Note the following: Karen Horney, *Neurotic Personality of Our Time* (New York: Norton, 1937), pp. 21–3, and *Our Inner Conflicts* (New York: Norton, 1945), pp. 161, 241–2; Theodore Reik, *Of Love and Lust* (New

York: Grove Press, 1959), p. 194; Karl Menninger, *Love Against Hate* (New York: Harcourt, Brace, 1942), pp. 292–4.

[19] Plato, *Republic*, vii. 521.

[20] Fromm, *Escape from Freedom*, pp. 143–4, 151–9.

[21] *Ibid.*, pp. 168, 173.

[22] Horney, *Our Inner Conflicts*, pp. 192–207; also see *Neurotic Personality of Our Time*, pp. 270–1.

[23] Karl Menninger, *Man Against Himself* (New York: Harcourt, Brace, 1938), Part III, Chapter 1, note 18.

[24] Friedrich Nietzsche, *Beyond Good and Evil*, Article I, Section 14.

[25] Herbert Marcuse, *Eros and Civilization* (Boston: The Beacon Press, 1955), Epilogue.

[26] Benedict, *Patterns of Culture*, pp. 23–4, 237.

[27] *Ibid.*, pp. 12–13, 233–7.

[28] J. Shields, *Monozygotic Twins* (London: Oxford University Press, 1962).

[29] William March, *The Bad Seed* (New York: Rinehart, 1954).

[30] Robert L. Katz, *Empathy: Its Nature and Uses* (New York: Free Press, 1963), p. 2.

[31] *Ibid.*, pp. 36–9.

[32] Benedict, *Patterns of Culture*, pp. 172, 173, 262.

[33] Katz, *Empathy*, pp. 136, 163.

[34] See: Marjorie Grene, *Dreadful Freedom: A Critique of Existentialism* (Chicago: University of Chicago Press, 1948), pp. 43–4; and John L. Mothershead, Jr., *Ethics: Modern Conceptions of the Principles of Right* (New York: Rinehart, 1955), p. 299.

6

Von Wright and the Naturalistic Fallacy

It is sometimes said that all a naturalistic thinker needs in order to make a case for objective or non-partisan status is to be allowed to identify happiness and good. It should now be evident that this is false. My attempt to make a case for non-partisan status in terms of eudemonic goodness involved two steps: first, identifying happiness with a form of goodness; second, utilizing an Aristotelian concept of good, or better, the three propositions hidden therein. *Both* of these steps are indispensable to my argument and therefore, anti-naturalists are likely to attack both, attack them as examples of the naturalistic fallacy. I will defend the latter step first in that it can be defended with brevity.

Recall my original statement of my Aristotelian concept of good, namely, 'there is a state for man analogous to overall health'. In referring to this as a concept of *good*, I may have invited the charge of committing the naturalistic fallacy. Certainly it seems arbitrary to identify the meaning of the word 'good' with some state of human functioning. Indeed, when we apply the usual test for the validity of a definition—that is, can we deny it without contradiction—our suspicions are increased. A man can say that a state analogous to overall health is *not good* and be guilty of no logical contradiction.

Actually, this argument is misdirected in that when I call the above a 'concept of good', I do not mean to identify it with what we mean by the word 'good'. It is *not* intended as

146

a definition at all. Rather, as we have seen, it puts forward a germinal concept, something that conceals a conceptual system made up of three propositions, and its purpose is to deal, not with a definitional problem, but with an epistemological problem, that is, the problem of objectivity. Aristotle states the problem it helps us to solve in these words: 'different persons have different, and sometimes contradictory, views of what is good. Clearly this will not do.'[1] Our Aristotelian concept helps us here by allowing us to distinguish the natural from what is merely conventionally good. Indeed, I call it a *'concept of good'* precisely because it is a *concept* which allows us to clarify the problem of the objective or non-partisan status of (eudemonic) *goodness*. But if the phrase causes anyone to think that it is a definition of the word 'good', I will be glad to drop it.

Aristotelians sometimes refer to the above state as 'the good for man', i.e. 'the good for man is a state analogous to overall health'. But here again, no definition is intended. Rather, they wish to emphasize that a certain state of human functioning, as distinct from happiness simply, is the good for man in a practical sense. Men are not angels who attain perfection by basking in the bliss of the beatific vision; men maximize their fulfilment by functioning in the context of a certain *way of life*. The point can be put in practical terms, that the man preoccupied with his own happiness has found a perfect formula for unhappiness, that one must genuinely love others, live for their sake, and let happiness take one by surprise.[2] Aristotelians feel the need to emphasize this point, for the fact they cite felicity as a justification of the perfecting life sometimes gives the impression that a man living this life would be motivated solely by considerations of his own personal happiness and thus, would be incapable of altruism. Nowell-Smith exhibits a clear grasp of what thinkers like Aristotle were getting at when he says that they were not[3]

> primarily interested in the question whether deontological words could be analyzed in terms of 'merely empirical' or 'natural' concepts. They believed that, human beings being what they are,

there are certain types of activity that are in fact satisfactory to them and that it is possible empirically to discover what these are.

*   *   *

However, all of this is not to say that Aristotelians can avoid supplying definitions of the word 'good'. For the first of our propositions about human nature utilizes one of the forms of goodness, that is, it asserts that a certain way of life is best for man in terms of happiness or eudemonic goodness. Which meant that when attempting to elucidate the meaning of this proposition, I had quietly to assume the validity of two definitions. It is now time to state them explicitly: (1) That the word 'happiness' exhausts the meaning of a *certain way* in which the word 'good' is used; and (2), that happiness can be defined as having broad and vivid fulfilling experiences and a harmonious emotional world. These two statements *are* genuine attempts at definitions. And since the 'deny without contradiction' argument is intended to test the adequacy of definitions, it is upon *them* (rather than my concept of good) that this test should be focused.

Let us spell out this test a bit more fully. Mary Warnock has emphasized the similarity of the methods used by G. E. Moore and A. J. Ayer to discover cases of the naturalistic fallacy.[4] Ayer points out that 'it is not self-contradictory to say that it is sometimes wrong to perform the action which would . . . cause the greatest happiness' and therefore, concludes that 'X is felicitous' cannot be equivalent to 'X is good'.[5] If 'felicitous' and 'good' were equivalent, it *would* be contradictory to deny that they were, just as it would be contradictory to say 'X is a woman, but X is not a female human being'. Moore dismisses the view that we can identify 'pleasure' or 'happiness' with 'good' by pointing out that we can ask 'is pleasure good?' and be asking something significant.[6] While if 'happiness' and 'good' were equivalent, such a question would be silly, would be like asking 'is a woman a female human being?' In my opinion, Moore's formulation of this test is more satisfactory than Ayer's, but I will use the two interchangeably throughout this chapter.

Here we begin to appreciate the significance of von Wright's work in distinguishing a variety of forms of goodness. It allows him to answer Moore's argument as follows: The fact we cannot identify 'happiness' and the *undifferentiated* word 'good' does not mean that it is a mistake to identify 'happiness' and a *particular usage* of the word 'good'. That we cannot *always* identify these two words merely shows that there are a variety of forms of goodness, a variety of fundamental ways in which the word 'good' can be used, and that 'happiness' can be identified with *only one* of these and *not* with the others. In other words, the reason we can ask 'is happiness good?' and be asking something significant is simple enough: we can be asking whether something that is *eudemonically* good (maximizes happiness) is also good in terms of one of the other forms, e.g. whether it is also *morally* good. Asked with that in mind the question is significant; but *then* it fails to show that happiness is not identical with a form of good. And if the question is used to try to show that happiness is not even identical with a form of good, with eudemonic goodness, *then* it becomes senseless; it makes no sense to ask 'is happiness eudemonically good?'[7] Nor can one deny that happiness is eudemonically good without contradiction.

I think that von Wright's reply to Moore and Ayer (by implication) is quite sound, indeed, I would like to put forward a supporting argument. If it is mistaken to believe that the 'question with significance' or 'deny without contradiction' objections work only because there are a variety of forms of goodness, then an opponent ought to be able to deny *all* the forms of goodness *collectively* without contradiction. He ought to be able to assert: 'I say that X is good, but I do *not* mean that X is moral, or felicitous, or pleasant, or healthy, or beneficial, or useful, or skilled, or working right, and so forth (until all the forms of goodness, and combinations of forms, are exhausted).' However, if someone were to make such an assertion, I think that we would be tempted to ask : 'If "X is good" does not mean any of these things, what the devil does it mean?'

There seem to me to be two effective counters to my supporting argument. First, an opponent might argue that the various forms of goodness have something significant in common and that therefore, the word 'good' can refer to something significant (this shared thing) without referring either to any one of the forms or to the forms collectively. Further, he might urge that whenever we judge something to be good we do so in terms of this shared thing ; and therefore, that none of the so-called forms of goodness are really identical with the word 'good' at all, that is, the felicitous, the pleasurable, the morally good, etc., are merely things which we judge to be good or bad in terms of our fundamental usage of the word 'good'.

In answer, I grant that all the forms of goodness *do* have one thing in common in that they are all *value judgments* of various sorts. But this shared characteristic is hardly very significant. For, as we go from one form to another, the *sort* of value judgment being passed is so very different; for example, eudemonic judgments assess things in terms of whether they are felicitous or fulfilling, while moral judgments assert that an act is intrinsically good with whether or not it is felicitous (to the actor) being entirely beside the point! In fact, the sort of value judgment passed as we go from form to form is so different that the shared characteristic, being a value judgment, remains in no real sense the same thing. Or better, we *never actually judge* something to be good simply, rather we always judge something to be good in the sense of one of the forms, to be eudemonically or morally or hedonically good, etc. And therefore, what the forms have in common, being value judgments, is *non-functional* in that we never pass a 'pure' value judgment on anything. Colours provide a helpful analogy. Colours have in common the fact of being colours. But as we go from red to green to blue, this 'shared characteristic' alters so much that it would have to be described as a *chameleonic* colour, which is another way of saying that it does not really remain the same thing at all. In other words, what colours have in common, being colours, is *non-existential*. We never actually find colour simply; we find only red or green or blue.

If 'shared goodness' is non-functional, if we never judge anything to be good simply, we can hardly treat the forms of goodness as things to be judged in terms of 'shared goodness'. Indeed, it seems to me that the *very thing* which the forms of good have in common, that they are all basic types of value judgments, is what *makes* them forms of goodness. It is in *terms of them* that we judge things to be good or bad and therefore, they are *not like* things to be judged, any more than Moore's 'goodness itself' was a thing to be judged; rather, it was because a thing possessed 'goodness itself' that *it* was good! Again, I grant that what is good in terms of one of the forms may be judged bad in terms of another. But no particular form has an obvious advantage here, some sort of claim to be the 'fundamental' form. Just as a Calvinist might consistently judge the felicitous harshly in terms of moral goodness, so others might judge the Calvinist's morality harshly in terms of eudemonic goodness, might accuse it of taking all the joy and spontaneity out of life.

A second counter to our thesis, that the forms collectively can exhaust what we mean by the word 'good', might well begin by conceding that point. However, an opponent pursuing this line of attack would go on to argue that if one takes the forms seriatim, what *each* of them means cannot be exhaustively defined in terms of human experience, or that this is true for at least some of them. To be more specific, even granted that happiness is identical with a form of goodness, is it legitimate to hold that a certain pattern of experience is what we mean by the word 'happiness'? Is this still not a version of the naturalistic fallacy, a matter of holding that a certain evaluative word can be defined wholly in non-evaluative terms? In dealing with this objection, I would like to point out that it is essentially an attack on my *second* definitional statement listed above, an attack on my attempt to define happiness in terms of a certain

11

pattern of experience, in terms of possessing broad and vivid fulfilling experiences and a harmonious emotional world.

Defending my definition entails developing a point touched on in the last chapter: men use the word 'happy' in a myriad of ways, many of which have nothing to do with assessing the merits of alternative ways of life. For example, they sometimes use it to signal a willingness to do something ('we shall be happy to put you up'); they sometimes use it as a synonym for good fortune or good luck ('that was a happy turn of events'); and so on. It is primarily *when* they assess a change (or a prospective change) in their way of life that men begin to talk in my terms. That is, they tend to say something along these lines: that they have discovered a new fulfilment, e.g. 'I have learned to enjoy poetry', an increase in *breadth*; or that the tenor of their emotional life has changed, e.g. 'I no longer feel at war with myself', an increase in *harmony*; or that certain fulfilments excel in *vividness*, e.g. 'I am told beatitude makes other joys seem pale by comparison'. The point is this: my definition must *not* be measured against uses it is not intended to elucidate. It was designed with a *certain usage* in mind, the sort of usage which concerns us as students of ideological appeals— appeals urging mankind to adopt a new way of life. The task of developing a series of definitions to cover all uses of the word 'happy' is an important one, but it is not ours.

Keeping the above qualification in mind, I am content to see the 'deny without contradiction' argument applied to my definition, which would, I presume, take the form of a question along these lines: 'Can anyone assert that he has no more breadth or vividness of fulfilment than he used to have, and further no more harmony of soul, and yet also assert that he is happier?' In applying this test to my definition, it is important to remember that the three factors which make up happiness are functionally inter-related. Certainly a man who has changed his way of life could say that he is happier today despite a decrease in *one* factor if this decrease has meant an increase in one or both of the *other two*. A dilettante might do well to take a loss in breadth of fulfilment to achieve a gain in vividness and harmony. And recall how the Kwakiutls and Zunis suffered from overemphasis on one factor; the Zunis might do well to sacrifice some harmony of soul in order to gain in the breadth and vividness of their fulfilments. But note that none of these examples force us to abandon talking in terms of our three factors.

*   *   *

Let us leave the 'deny without contradiction' argument behind and focus on the more general objection that human experience just *cannot* exhaust the significance of a value judgment. This objection goes astray by overlooking certain phenomenological facts, namely, that *certain* experiences stand out *precisely because* an inarticulate value 'judgment' resides in their very texture. Recall our contention that certain experiences are 'findings': that a man who thrills to a concert *finds* it pleasurable (hedonically good); that a man who experiences happiness *finds* his life fulfilling (eudemonically good), that is, the very tenor of his emotional life hums 'life is good'; and that even the experience of moral revulsion can be a *felt judgment* that an act should not be. This is *not* to deny that we can state value judgments without possessing these experiences *at the time*; that would be a very different contention from mine and a false one. Of course we can say 'that is morally wrong' and be saying something perfectly intelligible (that something is intrinsically bad) even though we are not at that moment feeling moral revulsion. Nor am I saying that without the above experiences, men would never have been able to make value judgments; this may be true, but again it is a different contention than mine. I assert this: that just as sense experience allows us to state factual propositions without illegitimately jumping some logical gap, so experiencing happiness allows us to state a eudemonic judgment *without leaping a logical gap*. The happiness of a happy man *passes* a judgment on his life, however inarticulate; when he says

'I am happy', this formal judgment merely *reports* the eudemonic judgment already passed. Thus, such a sentence *can* both report experienced happiness and communicate a value judgment; it is not a case of using a non-evaluative expression to express an evaluation.

My contention will probably not win assent easily. Our opponent would probably attack us along these lines: 'Even granted that happiness is experienced and even granted that it is an experience which includes an inarticulate value judgment, still there is a difference between a genuine value proposition and a proposition that talks about the occurrence of such experiences. For the latter is merely a proposition *about* the occurrence of (eudemonic) value judgments, a *descriptive* proposition *about values* (about eudemonic goodness). Take your identification of the value proposition "the humane life is eudemonically best" with the proposition "whenever men live the humane life, they find it most felicitous". Certainly, this latter is merely a descriptive proposition about the (eudemonic) values of mankind, indeed, it is a proposition of empirical psychology. Your analysis of the significance of value propositions reduces *ethical* propositions to *psychological* propositions.'

In passing, I wish to note that our opponent, in objecting that propositions *about experienced happiness* are propositions *about eudemonic goodness*, does not deny that happiness is experienced or that happiness is equivalent to a form of goodness; rather, his very objection equates experienced happiness and eudemonic goodness. Therefore, this objection seems to me logically distinct from the ones considered thus far, that is, it is not strictly an accusation that I have committed the naturalistic fallacy.

Against this objection, I contend that a proposition which talks about the occurrence of experiences *can* be merely a psychological proposition, but that it *need* not be. Such a proposition can be used as either an ethical or a psychological proposition and thus, we can still draw the line between ethics and psychology *while* restricting ourselves to propositions about the occurrence of experiences. I feel the need for a final analogy here. Consider a man who says, 'Whenever I look through this telescope, I see Mars with two moons', a proposition about the occurrence of visual experiences. Now it is possible that this man is in the clutches of a wild wag of an oculist who uses a telescope trained on Mars to test his patients' eyes (rather than an eye chart); in these circumstances, the man's statement is meant to assert that his eyes are functioning properly and it is a *biological* proposition. However, it is also possible that this man is in an observatory and has just discovered the second moon of Mars; in this case, his statement is about the existence of a heavenly body and it is a proposition of *astronomy*. Thus, although the proposition is about the occurrence of visual experiences, we have *not* been rendered unable to draw a line between astronomy and biology, for there is a real difference between a proposition *about what a man sees* and one *about a man's sight*. We might make clear how we were using the above proposition by some such device as this: (1) *Concerning the number of Mars' moons*, whenever I look through this telescope, I see Mars with two moons (astronomy); (2) *concerning the state of my vision*, whenever I look through this telescope, I see Mars with two moons (biology).

Now consider a man who says, 'Whenever I contemplate wanton murder, I find it morally repugnant'. He could be either telling someone about his views on the morality of murder, talking *ethics*, or telling his psychiatrist what sort of a man he is, that is, describing his *psychological* make-up so as to aid his analyst; and this *despite the fact* that we have restricted him to a proposition about the occurrence of experiences (in this case, experiences of moral revulsion). We might clarify the distinction as above: (1) *Concerning the moral value of wanton murder*, whenever I contemplate it, I find it morally repugnant (ethics); (2) *concerning me*, whenever I contemplate wanton murder, I find it morally repugnant (psychology). Similarly a man who says, 'Whenever men live the humane life, they find it most felicitous' can either be talking about the *eudemonic value* of a certain way of life for mankind or about mankind's *psychology*. And again, to signal the difference : (1) *Concerning the eudemonic goodness of the humane life*, whenever men live it, they find it most felicitous (ethics) ; (2) *concerning what men are like*, whenever they live the humane life, they find it most felicitous (psychology). And thus, although the proposition is about the occurrence of evaluative experiences (experiences that include an inarticulate value judgment), we are *still* able to distinguish ethics from psychology, for there is a very real difference between a proposition *about what men value* and a proposition *about men's values.**

To sum up : one can express a value judgment without reporting the occurrence of evaluative experiences ; and one can report the occurrence of evaluative experiences without expressing a value judgment. But still, one *can* report the occurrence of certain evaluative experiences (say that you have had a pattern of broad, vivid, and harmonious fulfilling experience—a pattern of experience that has passed an inarticulate value judgment on your life, that has made you aware that *your life is eudemonically good*) and be expressing the value judgment which those experiences have passed (be saying that *your life is eudemonically good*). There is *no logical gap* between the value judgment you are trying to express and the value judgment that your experience has passed as it has occurred, indeed, the former merely expresses the latter.

---

* Note that while the eudemonic example above refers to the evaluative experiences of third persons, the moral example is in the first person, that is, it refers only to the experiences of the speaker. This is not accidental in that propositions about the evaluations of third persons are *not* genuine *moral* propositions; the question of the significance of the first person–third person distinction for *eudemonic* propositions will be taken up at the end of this chapter.

Another point: I was tempted to exclude a moral example entirely. At times, I feel that moral experiences do not *quite* capture the *full* message of moral assessments. If true, this would mean that even a first person proposition about the occurrence of moral experiences does not express the full meaning of a genuine moral proposition. However, since I do not claim to be able to use an empirical approach to make a case for objectivity in terms of moral goodness, I will not elaborate on this.

This last seems to me of primary importance and prompts me to add a word for the unconverted. It convinces me that even those who think I am mistaken about the problem of *meaning* should not conclude that they can ignore my main contention. For what preoccupies me in this work is an epistemological problem, a problem of *truth*. My main contention is this: even if reporting the occurrence of experiences and expressing a value judgment are always two different things, *when* one *does* express a eudemonic value judgment certain evaluative experiences can vouch for *its truth*; the *reason being*, to repeat, that there is no logical gap between the judgment you are expressing and the judgment your experiences have passed. After all, there are subtle differences between making a statement of fact and reporting the occurrence of sense experiences. But despite this, we feel we can use sense experience to vouch for the truth of factual propositions. Thus, while I might concede that there are similar differences in the realm of eudemonic goodness, I would deny that they have *epistemological significance*. We can still use what men find felicitous (eudemonically good) to vouch for propositions about what is (eudemonically) good for mankind.

*   *   *

I will close this chapter with a very brief examination of two points which are related to our last objection, related in that neither is strictly identical with the charge that the naturalistic fallacy has been committed and both have to do with the line between ethics and psychology.

Von Wright makes an interesting point by drawing a distinction between first person–present tense value judgments and all others. He contends that *only* the former are *genuine* value judgments and he does this, not only in the realm of moral goodness, but also as far as hedonic and eudemonic goodness are concerned. In other words, von Wright holds that a man who says 'I am happy' or 'I like my life' is *actually expressing* a value judgment, but that a man who says 'I was happy as a child' or 'he enjoys his life' is not—rather the latter is merely telling us *about* someone's valuations.[8]

The above contention is well taken in regard to moral goodness; however, we are concerned with the realm of eudemonic goodness. Even here, von Wright's distinction is a useful one: there is always a significant difference between a proposition in which a man tells us what *he* finds good at this time and propositions *about* what men value or what men would value or what men would value most. But calling only the former 'genuine' value judgments troubles me in that it might lead someone to conclude that the latter are not central to ethics (a conclusion von Wright does not draw). For I believe that this distinction does not threaten my conclusion that certain propositions *about* values are ethical propositions. Certainly, ideological disputes are central to political ethics and yet, as we have seen, these disputes can be resolved *only* by propositions about what way of life men would value most (eudemonically).

Actually, this distinction, between first person–present tense value judgments and third person or past or future value judgments, helps to clarify our analysis of the re-solvability of value disputes. Recall the dispute between a humane man and a Nietzschean about the value of their respective ways of life. Their dispute arose out of conflicting *first person–present tense* eudemonic judgments, that is, each disputant at that time valued his way of life and not that of his opponent. On that level, as a personal dispute, it was found to be *unresolvable*. (Setting aside the possibility that the Nietzschean might still be flexible enough so that we could tell him that his way of life was cheating him of maximum felicity in the future; because note that this would involve propositions about his future, as distinct from his present, valuations.) Their dispute was found *resolvable* in so far as it was an ideological dispute, a dispute about whose way of life possessed non-partisan validity (assuming, of course, that the human experiment really does indicate that the humane life maximizes the felicity of mankind). And such a dispute is essentially a dispute about *third persons*, for it is a dispute about what is best for uncommitted mankind, a class that may not even include the disputants. In sum, we found our 'first person–present tense' value dispute to be unresolvable and our 'third person' value dispute to be resolvable.

It would have been utterly futile, when trying to resolve the above ideological dispute, to have confined ourselves to first person–present tense value propositions on the grounds that only they were 'genuine'. Such propositions were just not relevant, while propositions about the valuations of third parties, about the valuations of mankind, were directly relevant. And if someone wishes to say that it was the 'genuine' value dispute that was found unresolvable and merely a dispute 'about values' that was resolved, let them. For me, the significance of the conclusion that we can resolve ideological disputes about the (eudemonic) value of conflicting ways of life is *heightened*, not diminished, by the fact that we can do this *even when* faced by partisans locked in an unresolvable personal dispute about the value of those ways of life. Indeed, the contrast between these two sorts of disputes in terms of resolvability is the *raison d'être* for much of this work.

The final objection to be examined is one usually posed by social scientists rather than philosophers. It points out that the value judgments of different men vary with their psychological type, that is, humane men condemn enslaving the weak while authoritarians approve of it; from this, it concludes that value propositions really have only psychological significance. In reply, it is sufficient to say that this objection would collapse ethics into psychology no matter what interpretation of the meaning of value propositions, naturalistic or otherwise, was offered; for no analysis of the meaning of value propositions can alter the fact that different men will make differing value judgments and will say so. Actually, the fact that men possess differing values has nothing to do with the problem of *meaning*. It poses the problem of *objectivity* in the realm of values, just as the fact that men have differing sense experiences poses the problem of objectivity in the realm of fact. As we have seen, the existence of an actually shared physical universe allows for a solution to the factual problem, while our three propositions about human nature, particularly the second, hold the key to the problem of objectivity in regard to eudemonic goodness.

So we have come full circle; this chapter ends as it began, focused on Aristotle's concept of good.

NOTES

1 Aristotle, *Nichomachean Ethics*, iii. 4. 1113ª. 22–5.

2 *Ibid.*, i. 8. 1099ª. 7–16.

3 P. H. Nowell-Smith, *Ethics* (Pelican Books, 1954), p. 182; cited by Mary Warnock, *Ethics Since 1900* (London: Oxford University Press, 1960), p. 136.

4 Warnock, *Ethics Since 1900*, pp. 87–8.

5 A. J. Ayer, *Language, Truth, and Logic* (London: Gollancz, 1936), pp. 153–4.

6 Moore, *Principia Ethica*, pp. 15–16.

7 Von Wright, *The Varieties of Goodness*, p. 85.

8 *Ibid.*, pp. 72–5, 98–9.

7

The Problem of the Moral Hero

If our three propositions about human nature have the philosophical significance that I think they have, then a certain way of life can have non-partisan validity, though only in terms of eudemonic goodness, not in terms of moral goodness. This means that partisans who make ideological appeals on behalf of the way of life they espouse, who claim that it is best for uncommitted mankind, commit no *philosophical* absurdity, although they may be entirely mistaken in their *social science*, in their views about man and what perfects him.

However, they *must* stick to the language of eudemonic goodness, or better, they must do so if they intend their appeals to be non-rhetorical. When they use them rhetorically, then of course the sky is the limit and they can utilize any form of goodness (moral goodness included) that promises to arouse men's passions. It is of great interest to note that statesmen, at least in their non-rhetorical moments, *do* tend to couch their ideological appeals in the language of eudemonic goodness. The phrase 'improving the quality of life', a synonym for increasing human fulfilment, is often used. For example, Mr Kirk recently asserted that certain lessons learned in New Zealand would do more to raise the 'quality of life' in Asia than sending soldiers to take sides in her civil wars. And of equal interest, we tend to suspect statesmen who issue ideological appeals in terms of moral goodness if they seem to think that we should attach non-rhetorical significance to what they say. The late John Foster Dulles was resented, not because he issued moralistic appeals (all statesmen do this for the benefit of their partisans—which is quite legitimate), but because he issued moralistic *ideological* appeals; that is, he addressed his moralistic appeals to all mankind and demanded that they be taken seriously by the uncommitted. The uncommitted instinctively knew that such appeals were really partisan appeals and not binding on them.

In a word, it took the genius of the ancients, particularly Aristotle, to appreciate the philosophical significance of eudemonic goodness or happiness, that it allowed one to distinguish the natural from the conventional, to distinguish what has non-partisan validity from what has merely partisan validity. And, to give credit where credit is due, it took the genius of Nietzsche to appreciate the philosophical significance of the fact that happiness *alone* among the forms of goodness allows for such a distinction, namely, that the *only* non-partisan praise which we can give the perfecting life must be in terms of eudemonic goodness, must be in terms 'beyond' morally good and evil.

*　*　*

The above bouquet to Nietzsche may strike the reader as disturbing—and it should. For the fact we cannot claim that our ideals have non-partisan validity in moral terms creates far more problems for humane men than it does for Nietzscheans. Two in particular stand out, the problem of the worthiness of our converts and the problem posed by our admiration for the moral hero.

Some fear that emphasis on the eudemonic virtues of humanism will do more harm than good. Let me try to state their misgivings: 'Assume that our way of life does lure men away from our opponents because of its eudemonic appeal; what sort of converts are they likely to be? Note that they have opted for our ideals for purely selfish reasons, because of their desire for personal happiness. Such men are hardly going to feel committed to our way of life, indeed, they will desert at the first sign of trouble. Worse still, even if no sacrifices are required, they do not really believe in our ideals, their motives for adherence to them are extraneous. They are like a man who marries a woman because of her money : if it runs out, so does he ; but even if it does not, he loves her for her money and not for herself.'

My response to this will blend several themes largely undeveloped up to now : (1) Every now and then, the practitioners of a way of life experience a crisis of confidence —and when they do so, many of them begin to assess it (*including* its moral code) in terms of whether it affords them personal fulfilment ; (2) if such men wish to gain the felicity of the perfecting life, they must actually begin to live it— they must alter their present way of life ; (3) if they change their way of life, *this changes them.*

All over the world millions of people are in rebellion against the limited eudemonic possibilities of traditional ways of living and traditional moralities. Men become alienated in this manner, not because of something like personal misfortune, but when they begin to believe that their way of life has a defect at its core. That is, people in general do not lose confidence in their way of living because things take a turn for the worse in some chance way, because of bad luck, or a pestilence, or hardships suffered at the hands of a foreign oppressor. But when they decide that their way of life *by its very nature* robs them of fulfilment, that they would not find it felicitous even if they lived it *under favourable conditions,* then they are likely to rebel—to argue that their lives leave undeveloped something worthwhile in the *nature of man.* I see no reason to think of such men as potentially unworthy converts. Look at those around us who say that the status and possessions oriented style of life in America leaves them feeling tense, drained, and profoundly unhappy.

However, when converts come our way, we must make

them understand a fundamental truth about human nature (actually they will probably understand it to some degree already): men do not achieve happiness by brooding about happiness but *by living*—men maximize their fulfilment by *practising a certain way of life*. Which is to say that those who feel unfulfilled must alter their relationships with others and undertake new activities, they must begin to build relationships based on co-operation and mutual respect and the development of their creative powers. In a word, men who wish to experience the felicity of the life of humane love and creative work must learn how to love and work! I urge no duplicity here. Humanists worthy of the name will tell mankind that the egoist who continually aims at his own happiness misses it and that one must learn to put certain things (people, work, ideals) ahead of oneself if happiness is to flower. For example, the mother who loves only herself and not her children loses the fulfilments of mother love (and so with other human relationships), the man who cannot put his work ahead of his pleasure never really enjoys it, the man incapable of espousing an ideal never experiences the thrill of fighting in a just cause. Now it may seem that our converts since they were alienated from their old way of life by its lack of felicity would be put off by our message, would be deaf to any appeal except the sterile one of 'seek happiness'. But the very sterility of this appeal is on our side—men want to learn *how to live*; therefore, if we say 'if you want happiness, you must forget it and attempt a new way of life', they are likely to feel that this makes sense and to listen. After all, they know that a *way of life* robbed them of fulfilment. Clearly then, it will take a new way of life to achieve it.

The above anticipates much of my third and last theme. When men enter into new human relationships, then new commitments, emotions, loyalties, and eventually ideals begin to develop. Living a new way of life changes them into new men, if they are still flexible enough to change. The difference between our converts and the man who married for money is that he is not changed by his marriage, or better, when he marries he does not (despite his vows) *intend* to enter into a new kind of relationship. He may get a surprise of course, that is, he may actually grow to love his spouse; but that is the sort of exception which helps to prove our thesis. In sum, a convert who attempts the humane life and finds himself developed by it as a person, who learns to love, to empathize with others, etc., is not going to leave us lightly. As he becomes like ourselves, we are very likely to find him fighting at our side. Those who criticize us for issuing eudemonic appeals *must not isolate* those appeals from what they are about, attempting to live the perfecting life; for it is *the latter* which finishes the task of turning men into humanists. And we ourselves must never forget what we are about. We should agitate among those who feel un-fulfilled and should endorse new life-styles, or reforms, or revolutions; but if these do not lay the foundation for humane personal relations and creative work roles, they cannot produce a 'new man' and therefore, we must regard them as incomplete.

Needless to say, the fact that the humanist must develop altruistic or moral motives to live the perfecting life does *not* mean that he finds no 'joy' in the happiness which attends his way of life—experiencing happiness *is* to find something felicitous. Nor does it mean that he fails to look upon his happiness as a justification of his way of life—the tendency of mankind to find his life good, find it more fulfilling than other ways of life, can serve as a powerful justification. The point is that a man does not have to continuously aim at something (i.e. eudemonic goodness) in order to consider it significant. An analogy may prove helpful here, because the situation of the humanist is far from unique. It is the athlete who exercises to win a competition, rather than someone who aims merely at keeping fit (at 'feeling better'), that usually attains the highest degree of physical fitness and the greatest sense of physical well-being; but this does not prevent the athlete from enjoying his sense of physical well-being or looking upon its as a vindication of his mode of training.

The critics of eudemonic appeals include a fair number of

moral philosophers; many of these tend to focus on moral goodness almost completely and dismiss eudemonic goodness as simply irrelevant to the problem of justification. I hope that the last few pages will do something to redress the balance. Indeed let us say this: all in all, I count the desire for felicity or eudemonic fulfilment, and by this I mean personal fulfilment, as one of the great civilizing *and humanizing* forces of human history.

Now for our other problem and this one runs deep. For it is a problem all humane men must face, whether they be converts or born to the colours, and it is a problem in which our lack of a non-partisan justification in moral terms is complicated by something else: the tension that exists between our eudemonic and moral ideals. As I have said, these two do not fully coincide in my own case and I doubt that they will coincide for any humanist. Certainly, in eudemonic terms, the humanist ideal is the life of humane love and creative work, the life that humanists believe does most to liberate man's full potentialities for fulfilment. And just as certainly, the highest *moral* admiration of the humanist is accorded to a man who lives a *different* sort of life—to a man who sacrifices his own perfection, who may leave aspects of his own personality undeveloped, who may even risk his sanity, so as to systematically devote himself to making the eudemonically perfecting life available to others. I refer, of course, to the life of the moral hero, a life that can hardly be called best in eudemonic terms, albeit that it affords a certain sort of intense fulfilment, namely, the sense of living a noble life.

And when we give the moral hero our highest moral praise, we have to grant that it is purely partisan praise. We have to grant that we can make no case as to why those who do not share our basic moral values should not despise him. How bitter to concede the sceptic this victory!

A word of warning however: we must not exaggerate the distance between the eudemonic and moral ideals of the humanist. As we have seen, the way of life which is *eudemonically best* includes many acts which are not *eudemonically motivated*. The perfecting life has a strong moral emphasis and its practitioners are quite capable of acts of self-sacrifice and even acts of heroism. The fact that the mother who genuinely loves her child thereby maximizes the joy she finds in her relationship with her child makes her more ready, not less ready, to risk her life for him ; the same holds true of humane men in so far as they genuinely love justice. Thus, in favourable social conditions, one can do much of the work of the moral hero, one can do much to make the eudemonically best life available to others, *while* living it oneself. For, in favourable social conditions, where peaceful and persistent efforts towards social reform promise real progress and the penalties for such activity are not over-whelming, a measure of heroism is all that is required.

Although I do not want to exaggerate the discrepancy between the eudemonic and moral ideals of the humanist, I also do not want to falsely mitigate the problems posed thereby. To say the least, social conditions are not generally favourable, in fact, the eudemonically perfecting life is not easily available for most men anywhere. The needs of social justice in New Zealand may require only the degree of heroism that living the perfecting life allows for ; but America requires more than that, Czechoslovakia much more, and in Vietnam the need is almost unlimited. Thus, the problem of the moral hero is not a matter that affects one or two humane men, who feel morally obliged to sacrifice their own potentialities to serve others, with the remainder left free to live the eudemonically best life. More than a few, albeit a small number, will feel called upon to become moral heroes. And more important by far, a much larger number will feel called upon to go *some way* beyond acts of heroism, beyond the sort of heroism which the perfecting life allows for, so as to deviate in the direction of the moral hero. They will not become full-blown moral heroes certainly, but they will try to strike a *balance* between their eudemonic and moral ideals—they may not aim as high as Gandhi, but they will follow a Martin Luther King. In effect, the fact that we cannot claim more than partisan status for the life of the moral hero is something that affects almost all humane men.

However, in dealing with this problem, I will focus for simplicity's sake on the life of the moral hero proper. To the extent that I can bolster his *esprit de corps*, I will have helped all of those who take a step or two in his direction. Which raises the question : what can we say by way of justification of the moral hero?

While we cannot justify (in non-partisan terms) the moral hero's way of life, we can justify the *ideal* that lends his life meaning. And this is most significant. For what the moral hero seeks is not a state of affairs in which men must live his life but one in which the eudemonically perfecting life is available to all men—it is *that goal* which inspires his sacrifices. So that others will not live as mere means to the ends of the privileged, he turns his life into a means to *that end*. And if making the eudemonically perfecting life, the life of humane love and creative work, available to all is the ideal that captivates the humanist moral hero, then in justifying *that way of life* we have, I think, performed an important service for his *esprit de corps*. We can say to him : the ideal you think best for mankind and sacrifice so much for, the life of humane love and creative work, is indeed the best—and best in a non-partisan, rather than a purely partisan sense !

Again, I would prefer to be able to provide both a non-partisan eudemonic justification of his ideal *and* a non-partisan moral justification of his way of life. But I really feel that the former is more significant for him, for his *espirt de corps*, than the latter. Once captivated by the ideal he espouses for mankind, the moral hero can usually find in his own sense of moral integrity, his own feelings about what he must do to live with himself, sufficient motivation to make his sacrifice. Thus, while a justification of his moral impetus is highly desirable, it may not be essential to his *esprit de corps—just so long* as his ideal is untarnished. But what if his ideal could not be justified, what if the life of humane love and creative work was not (eudemonically) better for mankind in a non-partisan sense than non-humane alternatives? This, I believe, would deal a crippling blow to his morale. Given a man who has sacrificed himself for an ideal, his life seems meaningful as long as his ideal appears valid; but if that goes, his image of himself undergoes a tragic change—he becomes someone who has suffered for his illusions rather than his dreams.

*   *   *

The fact that we lack a non-partisan justification in moral terms does more than limit the sort of justification we can offer the moral hero. It sets certain limits on our efficacy in ideological debate. Note that the moral hero, as we described him, was a man with *humane* moral values; thus, he posed only a special problem, that of the conflict between the moral and the eudemonic ideals of the humanist. But what of men who have strong *non-humane* moral commitments? Clearly they pose a more general problem—one that will not appear in its most acute form when we are dealing with someone like a Nietzschean. For a Nietzschean, while non-humane, is preoccupied with Dionysian joy, with eudemonic goodness rather than moral goodness. Thus, it seems best to select a non-humane opponent with Calvinist leanings, that is, someone whose emotional life is much more dominated by moral goodness than eudemonic goodness. As this description implies, our new opponent would be a 'Calvinist' only in the popular sense of the word, only in terms of his psychology as distinct from his theology.

We can easily imagine someone of this sort attacking us as follows: 'First, let us assume for the sake of argument that your ideal, the life of humane love and creative work, is eudemonically best in a non-partisan sense. You grant that men can assess what is eudemonically best in terms of moral goodness. When I assess the above way of life in moral terms, I find it wanting—and I find the life of the moral hero (who seems too preoccupied with the *happiness* of his fellow men) not much better. I hold up a very different sort of life as morally good, a life oriented around the performance of certain exacting duties. Further, my moral assessments dominate my life, while eudemonic ones play a much less significant role. Why then, should I adopt a humane way of life? It is *not* that I am like the Nietzschean at forty who was so rigid that he could not change without permanently undermining his felicity and who could therefore, justify a refusal to change in eudemonic terms. Perhaps I still can successfully alter my way of life and thus, your ideal is eudemonically best for me. But I *choose* not to do so——and I base my choice on moral grounds.

'A second point: does not your whole frame of reference for testing various ways of life, assessing them in terms of maximizing felicity, betray a humanist bias? It is characteristic of humanists to be concerned with maximizing human fulfilment. And thus, your so-called test really comes down to elevating humanist values into a criterion, a criterion which allows you (not surprisingly) to give the palm to the humanist ideal. This is certainly not the sort of framework a Calvinist would suggest. Indeed, from our point of view, your very preoccupation with eudemonic goodness is suspicious. Is this not merely a matter of assuming that felicity is the only really important form of goodness? Is it not merely a way of insinuating that the proper end of man is maximization of happiness, rather than moral perfection, a view we Calvinists are hardly going to accept?'

We can dispose of the Calvinist's first point with some dispatch——by conceding it. Given his strong moral commitments and the fact that they play a much larger role in his emotional life than does what he finds good in a eudemonic sense, we cannot resolve a dispute with him as to how he should live; which is to say we cannot resolve a *personal dispute*, a dispute about his own personal code and behaviour. He can quite reasonably refuse to choose to attempt the humane life.

But when we turn to the realm of *ideological disputes*, it is another matter. If the Calvinist wants to convert the unconverted to his way of life, he can issue moralistic appeals if he so desires. However, a humane man can issue equally passionate moral appeals and here, the two ideological competitors are on a par. They must both grant that such appeals are purely partisan and rhetorical as far as those genuinely undecided between them are concerned. While in terms of the other major form of goodness, eudemonic goodness, we have a decisive advantage (in so far as non-rhetorical factors count) since we can issue non-partisan eudemonic appeals. Again, these appeals will probably not upset the Calvinist much as regards his determination to live out his Calvinist life. But they ought to upset him in so far as he is an ideologue. After all, our advantage might well mean in the long run gains for our way of life and the death of his. It certainly means that we can be more honest than he about our ideological appeals—something that ought to be important to those preoccupied with moral goodness—and still hope to be effective. For, once he grants that *all* of his ideological appeals on behalf of his way of life are valid for mankind only in the sense that he and his fellow partisans set a value on winning over mankind, he will hardly get a sympathetic audience. It is *this peculiarity* of ideology (that no one but your supporters need take your appeals seriously unless you can make a case for non-partisan status) which makes our advantage over the Calvinist so significant.

We can imagine another sort of ideologue, a Marxist, who might object that his *esprit de corps* would not be undermined even if he were to grant all of his ideological appeals were purely rhetorical, that is, were significant only for his supporters or his *potential* supporters. He might tell us that history has given (or will give) the mass of men (all except a capitalist élite) values which strongly bias them in favour of his ideology and that therefore, they need only his rhetoric to be converted. Here we must distinguish two factors relevant to an ideologue's *esprit de corps*. Certainly, if you can convince yourself that almost everyone is really already on your side (or soon will be), you will feel that rhetorical appeals will prove enough to win them over. And certainly, it will be a boon to your morale to believe that the chances of *success* for your way of life are great. But even the most dedicated Marxist usually wants more than that. He wants to be able to show that the way of life he champions is *worthy of regard* by mankind—that is would be valid for mankind even if he were mistaken and history began to take us towards something else, let us say Fascism. Marx himself felt this need—note his attempt to show that Communism was eudemonically best for mankind in a *non-partisan sense*. That is, he thought man to be a 'species creature' whose full potential for fulfilment was freed only in a certain sort of society, a view of human nature quite Aristotelian in character if elaborated !

The Calvinist can always refuse to go in for ideological competition ; so much the better for us. His refusal will hardly disturb us so long as we feel that *we can* make a significant non-partisan case for our way of life ; and a case in terms of one of the two major forms of goodness is significant. My analysis should leave the humanist's *esprit de corps* considerably higher than that of the Calvinist.

As for the Calvinist's second point, his charge that my frame of reference for testing various ways of life (testing them in terms of maximizing felicity) merely elevates humanistic values into a criterion for justifying humanistic values, this must be answered. It is true that humanists often have been excited by the notion that a certain way of life can free man's full potential for fulfilment. But here again we must make a distinction, a distinction between the *content* of the humanist ideal, the kind of life humanists recommend, and the *claims* they traditionally make on its behalf, the claims they make in their efforts to justify it. The kind of life humanists recommend is one oriented towards humane values, a life oriented towards humane love and creative work. Like most men, they have tended to claim that their life was best in terms of a variety of forms of goodness, moral, eudemonic, and hedonic. As we have seen, only claims framed in terms of eudemonic goodness can have non-partisan status. I am not sure that humanists have really been prone to issue more eudemonic than moral appeals, but if they have it may merely reflect a sort of instinctive philosophical acumen, a suspicion that these appeals were somehow more valid in the *context* of ideological competition —or it may have been purely accidental.

At any rate, whatever reasons humanists have had for making eudemonic appeals on behalf of their way of life, this makes it not one whit easier to show that these claims have non-partisan significance, any more than the fact that Kantians or Calvinists are addicted to moralistic appeals helps them to convince us that *those* have more than partisan significance. My contention is essentially this : the task of the partisan humanist is to justify the sort of life he espouses, a humane one. That way of life must win out in terms of eudemonic goodness in the same way its non-humane competitors might win, by being *lived* and found eudemonically best. The fact that humanists have traditionally claimed a humane life would win gives it no head start. If we want to imagine what would be a matter of rigging the criterion by which we test humane ideals versus non-humane ones, imagine that we turned to a *humane* criterion as a test, imagine that we called various ways of life good in so far as they approached being humane. That *would* rig the test in favour of humane ideals (though note that the life of the moral hero would win—*not* the life of humane love and creative work).

But testing non-humane versus humane lives *in terms of eudemonic goodness* does *just that*—and it does not rig anything. The reason we think it does is clear enough : the fact that it is customary for humanists to *claim* their life will come out best in a eudemonic test, plus the fact that this has become central to their *esprit de corps*, make it easy to get confused ; these facts tempt us to think that the humanist has some sort of advantage when such a test is applied.

Even if humanists have been more prone to issue eudemonic, rather than moral, appeals on behalf of the humane life, this does not mean that eudemonic assessments dominate their emotional world rather than moral judgments. The moral hero is clearly as preoccupied with moral assessments as the Calvinist, although the content of his moral ideals is of course different. He would call the performance of a painful duty, or a sacrifice, or heroism, morally good primarily when it was intended to increase the fulfilments of himself or others. While the Calvinist, at times at least, would call dutiful acts morally good even when they have non-humane consequences. However, this merely indicates the difference between humane and non-humane moral commitments. As for the ordinary humane man, recall that even his way of life possesses a strong moral side, puts a strong emphasis on morally motivated acts.

Remember that the humanist is not alone in the stress he places on eudemonic goodness. Only the way of life he recommends is peculiar to the humanist; appeals on behalf of a way of life in terms of eudemonic goodness are available to anyone who cares to make them. Indeed, if emphasis on eudemonic appeals helped one validate them, the Nietzschean would fare far better than the humanist. Nietzscheans attempt to eliminate their moral feelings and rely exclusively on eudemonic appeals. But this gives them no advantage. The *real significance* of the balance in a man's emotional life between eudemonic and moral assessments has to do with the relative importance he will attach to a justification in terms of one form of goodness *vis-à-vis* another. Unlike most men, a Calvinist will attach little importance to a justification in terms of eudemonic goodness, at least as concerns the conduct of his personal life. But this has already been conceded. If all the Calvinist means is that a justification in terms of eudemonic goodness will have less personal importance for him than for the typical humanist, we grant that. Though again, he may become personally demoralized, if he is concerned about the viability of his way of life as an ideology, when he realizes that he can make *no* case for the non-partisan validity of his ideals.

Finally, to defend my own 'preoccupation' with eudemonic goodness, this does *not* signal an attempt on my part to insinuate that the proper end of man is maximization of happiness. As a humane partisan, I hold that the proper ends of a man's life should feature love and work. As for my own emotional world, I can live with myself only if I find what I am doing both morally and eudemonically good. Sometimes these assessments clash and, like most humane men, I sometimes choose the former. Nothing would please me more than to have centred my analysis around moral goodness as well as eudemonic goodness, to have been able to make a case for the non-partisan validity of the humane life in terms of both of these forms of goodness. But I just couldn't. I can see no way to justify my ideals in moral terms, either for personal reasons or to heighten the advantage of humane partisans in ideological competition. The best I could do was to make the case I did—and be frank about its limitations.

In other words, I focused on eudemonic goodness for one reason only: its philosophical peculiarity, that one can make a case for non-partisan status in terms of it. And I have tried to emphasize that this sort of non-partisan status is a limited sort, limited by the fact that it is formulated in terms of *only one* of the forms of goodness. Look at the concessions to the Nietzschean and the Calvinist; look at the concession concerning justification of the life of the moral hero. These would have been unnecessary if I could only have made a case for full non-partisan status, a case in terms of moral goodness as well.

It is now possible to offer a summary statement of what my analysis can and cannot hope to do. It cannot make a valid case for personal change for non-humane partisans ('partisans' in my sense, rigid partisans like our Nietzschean at forty); and it cannot make such a case for non-partisans (again in my sense) who have a strong anti-humane moral bias and to whom eudemonic assessments mean little (like our Calvinist). But it *can* make a case of great personal significance for the rest of mankind, the only ones who are in any real sense potential converts; which means that it shows where the decisive advantage in ideological disputes lies, with the humanist, the only ideologue who can issue a significant non-partisan appeal. My analysis cannot solve the problem of justifying the moral hero's life or, in passing, the daemonic artist's life, the life of the artist who sacrifices himself to an aesthetic ideal. They must turn to their own inner imperatives for support. But it *can* justify the eudemonic ideal of the humanist and thus do much to sustain the moral hero. And in doing the two things it can do, I hope that my analysis makes a significant contribution to the *esprit de corps* of humanism's great mass of supporters, and its few heroes, and that sizable group that falls somewhere between the two. As for the daemonic artist, we must leave it to a philosopher of aesthetics to justify his ideals.

Have we then, solved the problem posed at the beginning of this work, the problem of ethical scepticism? Our failure to make a case for non-partisan status in terms of moral goodness certainly forbids us to claim a full solution. But our success in making such a case in terms of one of the two major forms of goodness certainly saves us from being left on a par (in terms of justification) with a non-humane opponent. Therefore, I think that we can say this: our approach has pointed the way towards (for the empirical evidence could always go against us) something that can qualify as approximately a half-solution.

*   *   *

A last point. The fact that my neo-Aristotelian approach leaves the justification of humanism at the mercy of evidence may be deemed a weakness. Now it is true that the evidence could defeat us in two ways. First, as has been granted, an empirical study may falsify one of our three propositions about human nature, e.g. it may indicate that no particular way of life stands out as eudemonically best, as bringing those who live it to a higher pitch of felicity than other lives. In this case, the ethical sceptic would be right. Second, and far worse, our three propositions may be verified (which means that the sceptic is refuted—or half refuted), but the way of life that stands out as best may prove to be a non-humane one, e.g. the superman's life. In that case, Nietzsche wins and we have to grant that the humane life is inferior in status to some non-humane alternative!

In regard to this, I can only say that anyone who espouses an empirical test of objectivity must be prepared to win or lose. If our opponents *could not* win under our empirical test, it would hardly qualify as a non-partisan test—and thus, could hardly confer *non-partisan status*. Indeed, for our test to be non-partisan, it must meet two conditions: (1) Its concept of happiness must have cross-personal validity, the three factors involved must possess validity for our opponents as well as ourselves; (2) it must not *in itself* load the dice against our opponents, that is, there must be no reason *in advance of evidence* to conclude that their ways of life could not afford a broad and vivid and harmonious world of fulfilling experience. About the first condition, I tried to satisfy the reader on this subject in Chapter 5 (see pp. 129–36) and will not repeat my arguments here. Concerning the second, the trouble is that we already have a great deal of evidence about the effects on men of various ways of life and we find it difficult to put it out of our minds. Therefore, we associate certain ways of life with certain of our factors, Zunis with lack of vividness, Kwakiutls with lack of harmony, the hollow men of our suburbs with lack of both—in fact, these associations become so strong that the psychic price of certain lives seems set by logic rather than learned by way of (often bitter) experience. However, imagine we came upon an angel ignorant of human psychology and human history. If we gave him a description of the *code of behaviour* recommended in various ways of life, I doubt he would be able to predict (in advance of evidence) which one amongst them would excel in terms of the factors that make up human fulfilment. While if we gave him a test like 'the greatest good of the greatest number', he might well be able to predict a victory for a humane way of life.

Thanks to the above, our test can qualify as a non-partisan one. If it could not, it would be pretty useless in providing a justification in the event that the humane life does win! One just cannot have it both ways: one's empirical test cannot *both* provide a non-partisan justification *and* be such as to bar a victory by some non-humane alternative.

Still, the question can be asked as to what I would do if an opponent wins, a loathed opponent, someone like a Nietzschean—would I then attempt to become a superman of some sort? Speaking for myself, I would not. I am a partisan of the humanist ideal and there is little doubt in my mind that the attempt to become a superman would mean a demoralization of my whole personality, which is to say I am like our 'Nietzschean at forty'. But I *would* feel obliged to give up *ideological appeals* on behalf of the life of humane love and creative work! I would have to leave this field to the Nietzschean, for I could no longer honestly tell uncommitted mankind that my ideals were best for them. I would have to grant that my appeals were only partisan rallying-cries and that the Nietzschean's had non-partisan status. In other words, I would do *precisely what* I would demand of a partisan opponent if his way of life lost : grant that the game was up with my way of life as a serious contender in ideological competition.

It seems then, that my neo-Aristotelian approach is at no disadvantage compared to other empirical approaches to ethical truth, for *they too* must give the non-humane a chance to win. Thus, my approach entails no *unnecessary* risks. And as for non-empirical approaches, as for 'demonstrations' that the humane life is best, these may seem to guarantee objective status to humane ideals, but in fact the sense of security they offer is an illusion. Assume that a demonstration that the humane life is best is possible. Then assume that the human experiment shows that some other way of life does more to liberate man's potential for fulfilment, does more to give man a broad and vivid and harmonious world of fulfilling experience. What demonstration will retain its credibility in the face of *that*! The conviction that the humane life does most *in practice* to perfect man is what has always nourished the humanist credo. If it does not, the philosopher can pull as many demonstrations out of his hat as he likes for all the practising, committed humanist will care.

This last encourages me, as we draw to a close, to make one last effort to convince my fellow humanists of the significance (for their *esprit de corps*) of our three propositions about human nature. The *principal purpose* of my labours has been to isolate the empirical hypotheses about man on which the *esprit de corps* of the humanist depends. I came by our three propositions in an effort to solve the problem of ethical scepticism and therefore, I chose that problem as a path to lead others. This may have been a mistake. I know that there are those who find that problem less significant than I do ; and there will be others who feel that my propositions do not solve it. To them I say, let each of you ask yourself some questions, ask yourself what hypotheses about human nature you hold dear. For I am convinced that most humanists have a variety of reasons for wanting something like my three propositions to be true ; for example, most like to think that we can make men both humane and happy, most dislike the notion of any genetic barriers (of any significance) to the practice of their ideals, and so forth. Again, ask yourself what it would mean to you if some non-humane life were eudemonically best for mankind, or if some men were born to be non-humane, or if we could not empathize enough to know that our way of life was valid for others. What I am suggesting is this : the problem of scepticism aside, my three propositions constitute a sort of humanist credo, a collection of beliefs and claims close to our hearts. If so, whether they stand or fall against the evidence becomes crucial and a matter of agonizing suspense.

Note that this credo is not identical with what I call the humanist ideal, the life of humane love and creative work. Rather it consists of claims about that ideal, about the eudemonic value and relevance (for mankind) of that way of life. Granted that humanists value their credo, that they *want* something close to my three propositions to be true ; however, this does not bias the case I have built on those propositions for the non-partisan status of the humane life. It would bias my case only if it (wanting them to be true) were a prerequisite for the validity of my case—which it is not. Men need merely *believe* my three propositions to be true, perhaps reluctantly, perhaps much against their will, for my case to hold—at least in terms of eudemonic goodness. In other words, I call these propositions 'a sort of humanist credo' because humanists *both* believe them and want them to be true; but *only* the former is necessary for my case.

Well then, let us face up to the fact that our *esprit de corps* is at the mercy of human history. If worst comes to worst, if the light of evidence shows the jewel of humanism to be flawed, at least our approach has taught us where the real responsibility lies, with social science; and thus, it can save philosophy from gratuitously taking the onus upon itself by way of muddled thinking about the naturalistic fallacy. Also, recall that such an empirical approach opens up exciting vistas as well as depressing ones. It may be that man's open-ended experiment with various ways of living will uncover a glorious variant of the humane life, perhaps the life of the humane mystic, that does far more to expand man's emotional horizons than anything we can conceive of at present. Humanism may find itself vindicated and transcended, rather than discredited, by the human experiment.

*　　*　　*

In closing, I know that in trying to cover so much I am subject to attack on many points; an army that fights on all fronts is vulnerable on many. However, I wanted to demonstrate the number and complexity of the problems raised, both for philosophy and social science, by the challenge of ethical scepticism. And I wanted to make clear why so many deeply committed political activists find that challenge so agonizing. And finally, I wanted to try to convey the powerful, cumulative drift of the classical approach to these problems, to try to make you understand why, after 2,000 years, so many of us still hover about the shrine of the ancients.

Appendix: Note on the Phrase 'valid for him'

Although the following may not interest the general reader, I hope that it will have considerable impact on professional philosophers. It has not been consigned to an appendix because it lacks importance; rather, its importance is such that I wish to take no chances about its being buried in the text. Another preliminary point: despite the reservations expressed in the text, I wish to exchange the phrase 'valid for him' for 'good for him' for the duration of the following analysis. There are certain advantages in this (which will become apparent) and further, the latter is the phrase usually utilized by those whose arguments must be answered.

When one attempts to use the phrase 'good for him' or say that (for the sceptic) ethical truth is relative to the person, one almost immediately runs into a certain argument. The core of this argument is that we normally say something is good or true *flatly*, that we do not qualify these words with reference to what people feel or think, that we use them (in my terms) in an objective sense; and further, that if we pin a tag on them such as 'for him', we have either merely expressed their normal meaning in a misleading way or have fallen into an incoherent usage—all of which is to say that the usage I have proposed cannot be *both* independent of normal usage *and* coherent. Just to spell the argument out: (1) To say 'X is good for him' is equivalent to saying 'the proposition "X is good" is true for him'; (2) but all of this is simply a misleading way of saying either 'he thinks X is good' or 'he believes that the proposition "X is good" is true'—and note that in these sentences the words 'good' and 'true' are used *flatly*, that the tag *'for him'* has disappeared; (3) therefore, no coherent usage of 'good' or 'true' has been discovered which is logically distinct from using them in the normal sense, a sense not qualified by what men value or think to be true.

The proposition that the phrase 'good for him' is incoherent (if used as a genuine alternative to normal usage) poses an obvious problem for the author. It seems to rule out the sort of phraseology I need to express my views on the logical consequences of ethical scepticism. Indeed, it seems to restrict us in our assessment of those consequences, to coerce us into *contra's position*, namely: that the sceptic not only can but *must* claim that his ideals are good flatly and that the only difference which the lack of an external truth test makes is that their goodness is not demonstrable. It is tempting to say that this in itself discredits the above proposition, that such a proposition merely begs the question of whether or not the absence of an external truth test makes a difference in terms of the grammar of our value assertions. However, my opponents are unlikely to be convinced by such a rejoinder, leaving me, I fear, with the task of showing that phrases like 'good for him' can be used coherently. In order to do this, I must take a roundabout path: we must momentarily shift our attention from values to facts and we must compare two very different epistemological situations.

The first involves a universe which is familiar enough, the universe of sense experience which mankind actually enjoys. Now, in that universe, to add the tag 'for him' or 'for me' on to the words 'exist' or 'true' would *not* pose a coherent alternative to normal usage. For example, if someone said 'that tree exists for me' or 'the proposition "there is a tree over there" is true for me', we would be justified in telling him not to talk in such a misleading way. We would tell him that he must mean to say either 'I see that tree' or 'I believe that the proposition "there is a tree over there" is true'. Unless he was trying to tell us that he thought his sense experience was hallucinatory, in which case his assertion 'that tree exists for me' might mean 'that tree exists *only* for me'; but this would be equivalent to saying either 'I merely seem to see a tree' or 'I believe that the proposition "there is a tree over there" is not true'. In any event, if he is speaking coherently, he must be saying *flatly* that the tree exists or does not and that the proposition is true or is not. The reason he must restrict himself to such usage, of course, is that we live in a shared physical universe which provides an *external test* of the reliability or unreliability of sense experience. As we saw in Chapter 5, anyone stubborn enough (recall our man with astigmatism) to persist in claiming that his sense experience is veridical *for him* can be shown, by a man with 20/20 vision, that such a tag makes no sense; he can be shown that reliable sense experience is veridical flatly, e.g. that it can predict events for everybody.

The second epistemological situation will tax our imagination. Imagine a universe with the following characteristics: (1) Each individual possesses a range of sense experience whose content resembles what we actually have *with the exception* that it includes no percepts of other men or perceivers of any sort; (2) each individual *within* his realm of sense experience can draw a distinction between veridical and hallucinatory experience, that is, some of his percepts correlate with other senses (e.g. some visual experiences correlate with touch while others do not) and some of his percepts prove to be reliable predictors while others do not; (3) at a certain point in time, each individual becomes aware of every other, not by way of sense but telepathy— thanks to the fact that all of their realms of sense experience are similar in content (all contain trees, spatial and temporal orientation, events, etc.), they can communicate and come to know that their realms of perception are similar; (4) however, the percepts of one individual have no relevance to what goes on in the experience of another— whatever I experience may help me to place objects, anticipate events, etc., but when I relay accounts of my experience

to the next individual these do not help him in any way;
(5) I (a member of this universe) *choose* to treat the other
individuals in it *as if* they were real—I have no way of
testing whether the messages I receive are 'real' or 'hallucinatory', of course, but I choose not to ignore them and *do*
converse with their 'senders'.*

No doubt, the point of all of this is obvious. In this
situation, *if* I choose to communicate, my language will
include phrases like 'exist for me' and assertions that certain
factual propositions are 'true for me'; and these phrases will
be neither misleading substitutes for some other kind of
usage nor incoherent—rather, they will be the only sort
of usage which is appropriate. Indeed, if I spoke to my
interlocutors about certain *objects of perception* existing
flatly, they would always make the mental reservation of
adding a tag, of saying to themselves 'these things exist of
course for him but not for me'. It would be only in regard
to the *objects of telepathy* (i.e. those with whom I am com-
municating) that it would make sense to talk about anything
existing flatly. And if I insisted on attempting to speak of
objects of perception as existing flatly, if I forbade them to
add their tag, they would accuse me of incoherence.

However, my larger point is this: there is nothing
inherently incoherent about language such as 'exists for him'
or even 'true for him'—whether or not such language is
appropriate *depends on the epistemological situation*. Which
means that terms like 'coherent' and 'incoherent' merely
cloud the debate about whether such language is a viable
alternative to normal usage; for these terms imply that a

---

* I do not want to get sidetracked into a discussion as to whether these
individuals could *develop* a common language (and thus converse with one
another) given that they live in private perceptual realms. As we shall see,
such a question is quite irrelevant to the point I am using my imagined
universe to make. However, if this question troubles anyone, it can easily be
circumvented by some such device as this: assume that our imaginary men
originally live in a common perceptual universe (like the one we inhabit) and
develop a common language therein; then, one day they all wake up to find
themselves with private perceptual realms (as in my imagined universe) but
with the memory of their common language intact.

certain usage is dictated by the logic of the usage itself, instead of by whether it fits the epistemological situation we are trying to articulate. To quote Wallace Stevens (whose lines caught my attention in *Moral Practices* by D. Z. Phillips and H. O. Mounce[1]):

> They said, 'You have a blue guitar,
> You do not play things as they are.'
>
> The man replied, 'Things as they are
> Are changed upon the blue guitar.'

In sum, we must face up to the possibility that 'words as they are' are changed when played on 'a sceptical guitar'. We must admit the possibility of altering usage as we go from a situation with an external truth test to one without such, rather than ignoring epistemological differences to suit the 'logic' of normal usage.

Our flexibility must extend, of course, beyond the language of fact to the language of value. As the reader knows, my version of the universe of the ethical sceptic bears a striking resemblance to the universe imagined above: (1) The imagined realm of sense is like the sceptic's realm of value—no *external* truth test; (2) however, the imagined realm of sense has an *internal* truth test (each individual can distinguish what is veridical or hallucinatory *for him*)—which is also like the sceptic's realm of value in that the latter can use his basic values to test what maxims are *good for him* (he need not become a nihilist); (3) the imagined realm of telepathy is like the sceptic's realm of sense—there one can say certain things do exist flatly. Now, having offered this comparison, I want to make something very clear: its sole purpose is to make the phrase 'good for me' a *debatable possibility* in our attempt to find language to express the logical consequences of ethical scepticism. It is offered to *encourage* a debate on the consequences of scepticism (to prevent such a debate from being outlawed by a verbal veto), *not* as an argument in that debate, much less as a clinching argument. Let no one accuse me of arguing by analogy, of saying 'the sceptic's universe is so like my imagined universe that we must say his ideals are good for him'. I present my arguments against contra in Chapter 2 and none of them are based on factual analogies; they are based on an analysis of the logical consequences of the lack of an external truth test *within* the realm of value. I am fully aware of the dangers of factual analogies—it may well be that lack of an external test does not make the same difference in the realm of value as it would in the realm of fact.

Another qualification: returning to our imagined universe, it allows for a certain use of 'true flatly' not pointed out as yet. In its realm of sense, one must say either 'X exists for me' or 'the proposition "X exists" is true for me'; but in addition, one could say 'the proposition "X exists for me" is true flatly'. 'True flatly' *is* meaningful here, the proposition cited *is* true for everyone in our imagined universe. *However*, it is true for everyone *only in a certain sense*, namely: once telepathic communication is established in our imagined universe and once all of its member realize that the percepts of each member have no relevance for the others, they will all agree that (given the epistemological situation) it makes sense to assert propositions like 'X exists for me'. And a consensus of *this sort* hardly threatens my analysis of the logical consequences of ethical scepticism. Nothing would please me more than to secure general agreement that if we all do live in the sceptic's universe (if no external truth test is defensible), it makes sense to assert 'X is good for me'. Therefore, I have made only one adjustment in deference to this sort of use of 'true flatly', that is, for the duration of this note, I have replaced 'valid for me' with 'good for me' in that the word 'valid' is often identified with the word 'true'.

Our imagined universe also allows me to dispose of a second argument, one related to our first in that it too uses a verbal veto to restrict our assessment of the consequences of scepticism. It runs as follows: (1) When there is an external truth test, it makes sense to ask whose views are correct, e.g. it makes sense to ask which of two astronomical theories is correct because we can test them against our observations of the heavens; (2) but when there is no external truth test, such a question makes no sense—e.g. in ethics, we can decide what is right and wrong within our own system of values but, when faced with someone whose basic values conflict with ours, it makes no sense to ask 'whose basic values are correct?'; (3) and since *such a question* makes no sense, it is senseless to answer it; (4) which means it is senseless to give a *negative answer*—to say that my basic values are somehow *not* (flatly) correct, to say that they are merely 'good for me'. In sum, it is argued that lack of an external truth test (what I call ethical scepticism) does not entail 'good for me' but rules it out!

The above argument resembles our first in another way, that is, it seems to me to beg the question of what scepticism entails. It gains its force from the fact that absence of an external truth test *does* rule out some sort of 'negative' wording, the sort of wording we would apply to an ideal if it had flunked such a test (for certainly, an ideal cannot flunk something which is non-existent). But the real question is this: *what sort* of wording is the logical correlate of having flunked an external truth test? The argument under discussion assumes that 'my ideals are merely *good for me*' is the only conceivable candidate; but I have proposed another candidate, namely, 'my ideals are *not even good for me*'. And therefore, we must debate which of these is ruled out and if it is the latter, the former is still in contention as appropriate in an epistemological situation in which there is no external truth test. In other words, I contend that it is the language of nihilism, not the phrase 'good for me', which is senseless in this situation.

However, setting all of this aside, our imagined universe allows us to dispose of the above argument with dispatch. For that universe lacks an external truth test *and yet*, it still makes sense to use the tag 'for me', to say 'X exists for me' and 'the proposition "X exists" is true for me'! And thus, the above argument cannot be valid as it stands—it cannot be valid to contend that lack of an external truth test *in itself* rules out the tag 'for me'. It is true that lack of such a test in our imagined universe makes it senseless to pose the question 'whose factual propositions are correct?' But the claims it rules out about objects I perceive are 'X exists *flatly*' and 'X does *not even exist for me*'—indeed, it leaves 'X exists *for me*' as the only appropriate alternative. Which is significant. For surely pro and contra agree that lack of an external truth test renders it senseless to pose *the question* of whose basic values are correct; what they debate is the sort of *claims* one can make in the absence of such a test. And again, I wish that debate to be an open one: just as I do not hold that lack of an external truth test in itself rules out 'good flatly', I reject the notion that this in itself rules out 'good for me'; the issue can be decided only after exploring what lack of such a test means *in the context* of mankind's universe of value.

Refuting our second argument pleases me for a number of reasons. For one thing, it has always struck me as peculiar that one had a right to ask for a full-dress debate on the consequences of ethical scepticism *only if* one could show that scepticism was false! It always seemed unreasonable that I had to present an external truth test in ethics to get the right to discuss what *lack* of such a test entails. For another, the reader can now clearly see that the two halves of this book stand or fall separately. Even if my case for non-partisan status (in eudemonic terms) is fallacious or worthless, my assessment of the consequences of scepticism might be valid—the latter is just not dependent on the soundness of my case. And equally important, the reverse is also true. Those who disagree with me about the consequences of scepticism, those who think all scepticism entails is that ethical truth is not demonstrable, may find my case of interest; they may value it as pointing the way towards the humanist having some sort of *demonstrable advantage* in ideological debate. Which is something that all humanists, whatever their philosophical persuasion, would (I hope) welcome.

Having said that, I will content myself with reiterating

the purpose (the *sole* purpose) of this note. It is designed to show that phrases like 'exist for him' and 'true for him' (with a qualification) and 'good for him' do not suffer from some kind of incurable disease. It is designed to make us discuss an unpalatable proposition: that the language of value played on the sceptic's guitar takes on a new grammar.

NOTE

[1]Routledge & Kegan Paul, 1970.

Index